AGE IS NOT A HANDICAP

A COMPLETE GUIDE TO PLAYING GREAT GOLF FOR SENIORS

JAY MORELLI
with Photos by
BRUCE CURTIS

McGraw·Hill

New York   Chicago   San Francisco   Lisbon   London   Madrid   Mexico City
Milan   New Delhi   San Juan   Seoul   Singapore   Sydney   Toronto

Library of Congress Cataloging-in-Publication Data

Morelli, Jay.
    Age is not a handicap : a complete guide to playing great golf for seniors / Jay
Morelli. —1st ed.
        p.   cm.
    ISBN 0-07-144416-5
    1. Golf for older people.   I. Title.

   GV966.5 .M67   2005
   796.352′084′6—dc22   2004030514

1 2 3 4 5 6 7 8 9 0   DOC/DOC   0 9 8 7 6 5

ISBN 0-07-144416-5

McGraw-Hill books are available at special quantity discounts to use as premiums and
sales promotions, or for use in corporate training programs. For more information, please
write to the Director of Special Sales, Professional Publishing, McGraw-Hill, Two Penn
Plaza, New York, NY 10121-2298. Or contact your local bookstore.

This book is printed on acid-free paper.

Dedication

I have dedicated this book to Ted Kroll. Ted passed away in the spring of 2003. He was a golf champion and one of the most unforgettable men I've ever known.

Ted started his golf career by hitchhiking to the 1941 U.S. Open at the Colonial Country Club in Fort Worth, Texas. He had qualified for that Open locally in the Central New York section. He lived in Utica, and didn't have a car at that time, so he got a ride with another qualifier from Rochester. Ted's journey began by hitchhiking from Utica to Rochester, then driving to Fort Worth. This was a very modest way to start a brilliant golf career.

Ted joined the U.S. Army in 1941 and was sent to Europe. He came back with a wheelbarrow full of medals. He was one of the most decorated soldiers in the European theater, but in the 30 years I knew Ted, he never once mentioned that time of his life.

Ted became a premier player on the PGA Tour from 1949 to 1956. His best year was 1956, when he won three times and was the leading money winner on the Tour. He was the star after the Hogan period and just before the Arnold Palmer reign. As a matter of fact, Palmer's first victory in the United States was in a play off against Ted at the Hartford Open. (Ted had won the inaugural Hartford Open.) Just to show how times have changed, Ted left the PGA Tour the year after his best year, 1956, to accept a position as a club professional. Ted had a family: his lovely wife, Jane, and four daughters. There just wasn't enough money at that time in professional golf on which to raise a family. In 1962 Ted left his club job for a week to do a little fishing and win the Canadian Open. He still had what it takes.

Ted Kroll played on three Ryder Cup teams and had an outstanding Ryder Cup record. He was quite a man. It was an honor to know him.

CONTENTS

Foreword by Hubert Green   vii

Acknowledgments   ix

Introduction   xi

1	The Golf Swing	1
2	Course Management	21
3	Equipment	35
4	The Mental Side	41
5	Physical Conditioning	47
6	Nutrition	81
7	The Short Game	85
8	Putting	95

9   The Sand Game (or "Bunkerphobia")   105

10   For Women Only   113

11   The Myths of Golf   117

12   Practice Drills and Training Aids   121

13   Shot Making   135

14   Flaws and Fixes   139

15   Etiquette   143

16   Some Final Thoughts   147

Glossary   149

Bibliography   157

Index   159

Foreword

Jay Morelli and I played golf on the same college team at Florida State. We had quite a collection of good college players: Denny Lyons, one of the best; Bob Duval, David Duval's dad; and, of course, Bob's older brother, Jim Duval, whom we affectionately called "the elf." Jim Conace could hit the ball into orbit, and putt, too! Ron Philo was on our team. His daughter, Laura Diaz, is now one of the stars on the LPGA Tour, winning at the 2002 LPGA Corning Classic. Ron's son, Ron Jr., is one of the finest club professionals in the PGA. Another outstanding player was my good friend Smokey Keeney from Decatur, Georgia. About half of my teammates were from the North. Smokey and I, and a few others, were from the South. The natural match then was the "grits" against the "home fries." I'm not sure who won the majority of the matches, but I know we had more fun than the law allows.

While I chose a career as a professional golfer, Jay chose a career as a golf professional, specializing in instruction. We have both been very lucky.

You will really enjoy Jay's book on senior golf. He provides solid instruction and relays a ton of tricks he's learned through a long career and a lot of experience in the golf business. Read it carefully. These tips are simple. He didn't try to reinvent the wheel but just tried to pass on some solid golf sense.

—*Hubert Green, 1977 U.S. Open and 1983 PGA champion*

Acknowledgments

Our golf game is a product of our technique, our physical abilities, our strength, our diet, our state of mind, our equipment, and so many other factors. I've tried to touch on all these areas and present an overview of the game, with suggestions for improvement. I've needed quite a bit of assistance to cover all this ground. Thanks to Dr. Harry Haroutunian for his contribution on nutrition; Dr. Jack Graham, Marcie Himelson, and Larry Feldstein on physical conditioning; Dr. Alan Shapiro on golf psychology; Shaun Wheatley on equipment; and Keith Newell on etiquette and technical assistance. Thanks to Sue Stafford, Joan McDonald, and Sue Newell for their contributions to the "For Women Only" chapter. Thanks to Tom Joyce for supplying one of the best golf swings I've seen. Thanks to Plantation Golf Resort, Crystal River, Florida; Glen Oaks Golf Club, Old Westbury, New York; and Mount Snow Golf Club, Mount Snow, Vermont. Thanks to Dee Reynolds and the management at Black Diamond Ranch. Thanks also to my editor, Mark Weinstein, at McGraw-Hill. A special thanks to Christine Overton, who helped me organize the book. Without Christine, I'd still be on page 6.

Introduction

Golf is a multifaceted game that combines power and finesse. It requires us to be patient and keep our composure and, most of all, it's a lot of fun. Is there any greater fun than sinking a putt on the last hole to win a match and beat an old rival or friend? I think the best part of this elusive game is that you can play golf forever. It is truly a game for a lifetime.

Senior golf can be the most fun. Seniors normally have more recreational time as their families grow older and they approach retirement. This is the time to make new friends and enjoy old ones on the course.

The challenge is to play at a level that is still competitive. As athletes get older, their skills naturally diminish. That is a given. Golf is fascinating in that we have the opportunity to improve the finesse aspects of the game, which can more than compensate for the loss of some distance off the tee. A senior's best golf may still be ahead.

Here is a wonderful example of enjoying senior golf: Ted Kroll, to whom I have dedicated this book, was a friend of mine. Ted always enjoyed playing with other golf professionals, with a small wager in mind. Well, one fine day, Ted got to the local course to find a "good game." Ted at the time was about 70 years old. There were seven pros and Ted. The other pros were half his age. It was decided that one foursome of pros would play "best ball" against the other foursome. In deference to Ted's age, they allowed him to play the red tee markers, which are closer to the green than the blue markers the other pros played. Big mistake. For Ted, the shorter course more than made up for his loss of distance. From the red tee markers, Ted shot a 66 on his own ball and beat the other foursome of pros by himself. In doing so, he proved two points: one, that playing the correct tee markers makes it fun for all, and two, in Ted's case, that a thoroughbred is always a thoroughbred.

1

The Golf Swing

The fundamentals of the swing are the same regardless of age. This chapter reviews some of the fundamental concepts and suggests small adjustments that seniors can make to compensate for loss of strength and flexibility.

The Preshot Routine

The preshot routine is a ritual we perform before we actually swing the club. It sets the tone for the swing. A good preshot routine can help produce consistency and reduce tension. All golfers get nervous. Whether playing in the club championship, at the U.S. Open, or with friends, we all have times when we can feel the tension creeping through our body. When we're playing late in the afternoon with a good friend, the game can seem so easy; we're relaxed and good shots are automatic. When we're on the first tee in front of a crowd, we become tight; it appears impossible that the little white ball can end up in that little hole at the end of a very long fairway in a reasonable amount of swings. Is there a trick we can use to have that relaxed feeling all the time? Well, yes and no.

Nervous energy is part of competition and is also natural when a thousand spectators are looking at you on the first tee. A good preshot routine will help ease the tension and help you focus on the task at hand. The preshot routine should be consistent: it should take the same amount of time and include the same mannerisms every time. So often, we try extra hard in a pressure situation. In the attempt to get everything just perfect before we swing, we spend more time standing over the ball than usual. However, in that extra time, it is obvious that we are not going to become more relaxed. In fact, spending more time over the ball is a surefire way to get tighter in the grip and arms. This tension will produce a less rhythmic and weaker golf swing. Each golfer needs to develop his or her own preshot routine. I'll tell you what I do in my preshot routine.

First, I try to really relax my shoulders and actually let my arms go limp. I try to ease all the tension out of my body. Second, I stand behind the ball and visualize the shot I plan to play. I vizualize how high I want the ball to fly and whether I want it to curve to the left, curve to the right, or if I'm trying to play the most difficult of all shots, the straight shot. Third, I draw an imaginary line along the turf from the ball to the target and pick out a spot along that line—maybe a few feet ahead of the ball. That spot may be a small divot or a change in the color of the grass. The idea is to choose an intermediate spot at which to aim the clubface. For those who bowl, this is similar to "spot bowling," in which you aim not at the headpin but at a spot on the alley. This is the way to assure you are lined correctly at the target. Fourth, I aim the clubface at the target, using the intermediate target to get that alignment correct. Fifth, I place my right foot square to the line of the flight of the ball and then my

Set the clubhead behind the ball, aiming the clubface directly down the intended line.

left foot. Sixth, I establish good posture and get comfortable. And finally, I take three "looks" at the target by turning my head and changing my focus from looking at the ball to looking at the target, and then I swing.

The best players concentrate on the target, while the average recreational players stay fixed on the ball. Notice that the professional players really zero in on the target as they stand over the ball at address. They are totally tuned in to where they want to hit the ball. Recreational players often just focus on the ball and not the target. The great teacher Harvey Penick had a simple phrase: "Take dead aim." Perfect.

You're welcome to use my preshot routine, or you can develop your own. We all have our own speed, metabolism, and ways of doing things. We all need our own program, and you should develop a routine that works for you. A preshot routine may seem like quite a project,

Establish good posture and balance.

but the entire process should take only a few seconds and should have a rhythmic flow.

Once you have established your routine, stick with it. The routine will help put you in a "zone." The feeling of being "in the zone" has been described by many athletes as a state in which you're totally focused on the task at hand. You can see the results almost before they happen. You're not in any way tied up with technical thoughts about mechanics. A good preshot routine is the first step to getting in the zone. The consistent feel and rhythm will make the game natural. When it's done properly, almost all of the pressure created by the situation will disappear.

The Golf Grip

How you hold the club will affect everything in the golf game: the shape and look of your swing, the distance you can drive the golf ball, your accuracy, and your score. That's pretty important! If there is a secret to being a good golfer, it is to hold the handle of the club correctly so that you automatically achieve the most effective hand action. The correct grip will promote the wrists to properly "hinge" on the backswing to create power and unhinge on the downswing to release power. You notice how effortlessly expert golfers generate power. That power is a product of the correct grip.

To begin, let's talk about grip pressure, or how tightly you should hold the handle. Grip pressure should be soft. Most golfers hold the handle too tightly. You should hold the club with enough pressure to control the club but—and this is important—softly enough to feel the clubhead. Your hands and arms should be relaxed. For want of a better phrase, grip pressure should be a 2 or 3 on a scale of 1 to 10, with 10 being the tightest. Your hands can't work properly if the natural wrist action cannot take place because you're squeezing the handle too tightly. Holding the club with unnecessary pressure is work, but there is no job! Squeezing the handle is also unnecessary because the golf club weighs between 10 and 14 ounces and the ball weighs roughly an ounce and a half. The right grip is light work.

A tight grip will also inhibit some motion. Relaxed grip pressure will help produce speed and a free, swinging action, which translates to distance and accuracy. Again, if there is a real secret to the game, it's that a good grip creates a hinge in the wrists that will consistently deliver power.

So, with nice "soft hands," hold the club in your top hand (the left for right-handed players) so that it rests diagonally across your palm, mostly in your fingers. The handle of the club can easily

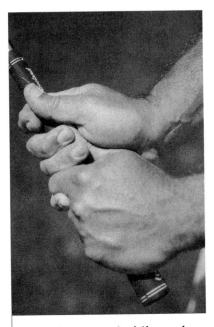

The hinge created through the proper grip will deliver power and consistency.

Hold the club in the top hand so that it rests diagonally across the palm, mostly in the fingers.

In the bottom-hand grip, the club is held more in the fingers.

be supported by the palm and forefinger.

When you close your fingers around the handle, a V will be formed by the crease between your thumb and forefinger. That V should point to your back shoulder if the club is held directly in front of you. If you do this properly, you will easily be able to feel and create a hinge. That hinge is the key to power.

For the correct bottom-hand grip, half close your hand so that a pocket forms in your palm. Place your bottom hand on the handle so that this pocket covers the thumb of your top hand. The V created by the thumb and forefinger of your bottom hand should also point to your back shoulder.

There are three ways to complete the proper grip. The first is to use the classic Vardon grip, in which the pinky of the bottom hand rests between the forefinger and middle finger of the top hand. This method of holding the handle of the club was devised by the great British player Harry Vardon, who thought that joining the hands like this was the most efficient way to deliver power and consistency.

The second way is to use the interlocking grip, in which the pinky of the bottom hand locks between the forefinger and middle finger of the top hand. For right-handed players the pinky of the right hand interlocks with the forefinger on the left hand. The hands are not in any way joined. Tiger Woods and Jack Nicklaus both have used this grip. Not a bad example to follow.

The third grip option is the 10-finger, or baseball, grip. All 10 fingers get to play golf in this style. The player holds the club much like a baseball bat, all 10 fingers hold the bat, or club, handle. The 10-finger grip is particularly recommended for players with small hands. With whatever style you use, your hands should work together as a unit, like one big hand on the handle of the club.

Seniors should check fundamentals to make sure they're getting the most efficiency from how they hold the handle of the club. For starters, check that grip pressure. A loss of power can be frustrating, and seniors often try to find more yards off the tee by holding on to the club too tightly. So, try lightening up the grip . . . a lot. It always will make the club feel lighter and freer. Over time, you may have developed the habit

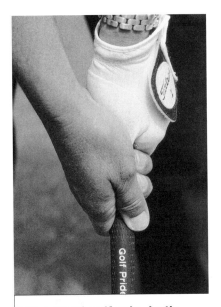

In a good golf grip, both hands are joined and look like one big hand on the club, both V's pointing toward the back shoulder.

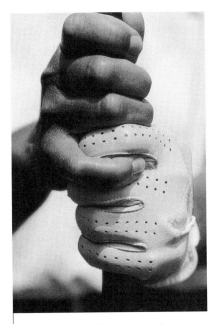

The classic Vardon grip

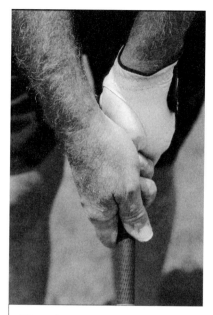

The classic neutral grip with the V's created by the thumb and forefinger of both hands pointing toward the back shoulder

of squeezing the life out of the club. If you have become accustomed to holding on too tightly, it may take some time and discipline to correct. Try holding on so softly that you feel you may throw the club down the fairway—it works!

You can also try experimenting with a new grip style. If you have had a Vardon grip for many years, try a few practice balls holding the handle a different way. A 10-finger grip, in theory, promotes the most hand action, and it is often worth experimenting with. The grip is the heart and soul of your game, and a change in the way the club feels may make a world of difference.

A final possibility involves changing the grip described earlier, which has both V's pointing toward the back shoulder. This is called a neutral grip. You can strengthen the grip slightly by moving your hands so that the V's point below your back shoulder. This is called a strong grip and will promote a draw or hook. The change should be slight, and if the result is not improved shots, it should not be made. A slight draw or hook will add a few yards to tee shots, but that's not worth the sacrifice of control or solid contact. Remember that solid contact is the most important piece to distance. (My good friend Jim Conace, with whom I played college golf at FSU, says, "Good players spend the first third of their golf life hooking the ball, the second third trying not to hook, and the last third trying to hook it again.") We all look for a few more yards as we get older. The hook will generally go farther than the fade, although it's harder to talk to a hook when it's headed toward trouble.

The Address Position

How we stand to the ball is called the address position. It has three parts: stance, alignment, and posture.

The first part is where you position the ball in the stance. Should the ball be opposite the front foot, the middle of the stance, or the back foot?

To generalize, the bottom of your swing is about in the middle of your stance. Because we transfer weight from the back foot to the front foot, the bottom of the swing is slightly forward of center. So, the ideal ball position for most clubs is just forward of the center of your stance. We take a wider stance with the driver than with the short irons, so the ball position with a driver may appear to be a little farther forward in the stance. Your feet should be shoulder-width apart with a 5-iron, a little wider with a driver, and narrower with a short iron. Longer clubs also require a more sweeping action than the short irons, another reason why the ball should be more forward. The point here is that the ball should be center to slightly forward in the stance with all clubs for a routine shot. (There are times when the ball position will change for specialty shots, such as when you are looking for a low trajectory into the wind.) The rear foot should be square to the line of flight. This will allow the hips to turn the correct amount. The front foot should be turned out about a quarter of a turn. This will help you finish the swing more easily. You can even try a small experiment to get the feel of flaring out your front foot: Stand with both feet straight ahead, and then turn toward the target. Now try the same movement with the front foot turned a quarter turn toward the target. You can instantly feel the forward hip pulling you around. It's the way we're built!

Second, alignment has to be correct. If the alignment is not correct, then only a compensating or incorrect swing can produce a favorable result. The incorrect swing will be reinforced if you're not aimed at the target. So, if the alignment is not right, and the swing is not quite right, the ball may go straight. The off-line swing becomes reinforced, and that becomes "your swing." A few compensations can create a few

In a good address position, the ball is played center to forward in the stance.

good shots. You can see how poor alignment can limit your potential as a golfer. There is a system to achieving proper alignment. First, align the clubface squarely at the target, set your back foot square to the line of flight, and then set your forward foot square to the line of flight. (The clubface is the absolute; it's what we hit the ball with. Many golfers try to set their feet first and then square the clubface, which is incorrect and confusing.)

Part of proper alignment is correctly "aiming" the clubface at the target. There are a few tricks to accurately aiming the clubface and then properly aligning the body. First, when you pick a target, choose the smallest possible spot. You're much better off zeroing in on a branch rather than the whole tree. A famous story about Ben Hogan illustrates this point. Hogan was playing at Seminole Golf Club for the first time. He came to a semiblind tee shot. He couldn't see the fairway and asked his caddy where to aim. There was a small cluster of palm trees beyond the fairway that most of the players used as a target. The caddy told Hogan to aim at those palm trees. Hogan, in his deadpan manner asked, "Which one?" While this is classic Hogan, it also reinforces the point that to be as accurate as you can be, you should focus your attention and alignment on the

smallest target that you can comfortably define. Second, as I mentioned in the discussion of my preshot routine, I draw an imaginary line from the ball to the target, whether it be a branch or the flagstick. Then I pick out a spot on the grass that is on that line. It might be a blade of grass, a divot, or a discolored area. Finally, I aim the clubface at the spot. Proper aiming and alignment cannot be underestimated.

Every now and then, you'll make a great swing and the ball will fly dead straight way off the mark. If you hit one like that, place a club across your toes at the end of the swing. My bet is that the shaft of the club will be pointing directly where that ball went, not at your target. While you can't replay the shot you've just hit, this can be a good learning experience. At least you'll know that the errant shot was a product of poor aiming and alignment and not a swing flaw.

Good posture is illustrated by a slight flex of the knees and some tilt from the hips. Notice that the arms are relaxed and comfortable.

The third part of the address position is posture. Posture is different things to different people. To a West Point cadet, it is standing as straight as a pole. To a golfer, it is getting into a good athletic position. If a golfer stands as straight as a West Point cadet, the spine will be vertical, and since the shoulders move around the spine, the spine must be at a tilt or an angle so the club can reach the ball and ground on the downswing. Standing up straight is great for hitting a baseball at waist-high level but is not very good if you're trying to hit the ball off the turf.

In order for you to comfortably be able to "reach" the ball in a golf swing, a tilt is absolutely necessary. You achieve the correct angle by tilting from the hips and pushing the hips back slightly. Pushing the hips back slightly will move weight from the toes to the center of your feet, where it belongs. A good test to make sure you have done this properly is to wiggle your toes in your shoes. In a good posture, the tilt will create a feeling of tension in your lower back. It takes some effort to achieve good posture. The tilt changes the angle of your spine. If you don't tilt, your spine will remain perfectly straight up and down. Proper posture will also keep the clubhead on the target longer. Think of it this way: Proper posture will help you swing the clubhead on a path that resembles a Ferris wheel, up and down; it will be on the right path during most of the swing. Improper posture, with no tilt, will produce a swing in which the clubhead is on a path that resembles a merry-go-round. The clubhead will get too far behind your body. It will be difficult to return the clubhead squarely and swing it toward the target.

Your knees should be slightly flexed, just enough "to let the air out." Too much knee flex will be unnatural and will create a starting position that is difficult to maintain throughout your swing.

In a good athletic stance your weight should be evenly distributed on both feet. A very important—but often overlooked—point is that the weight should be on the insteps of both feet, this will bring the knees together in a "knock kneed" position. This position will make your swing more rotational and prevent your weight from going to the outside of your back foot on the backswing. The width of your stance should be a few inches wider than your shoulders.

Seniors should carefully review their address position. It's easy to fall into bad habits, getting a little careless and sloppy. Poor posture will result in a loss of distance and consistency. The address position should be relaxed and comfortable. The arms hang easily from the shoulders. If the grip is correct, there will be a slight hinge in both wrists. Then a good shoulder turn will automatically put the club in the perfect position at the top of the swing. Good posture will also help you figure out how far you should stand from the ball. This distance is an easy measurement: if your upper arms can touch your chest, and you have the correct tilt, the club will be on the ground at the spot where the ball should be played in your stance.

There are some "senior adjustments" at the address position I'd like to suggest. Like all other adjustments, they may vary from standard golf instruction and should be tried as experiments. Some seniors lose mobility and flexibility. To compensate for less ability to transfer weight from the back foot to the front foot, try moving the ball back slightly in your stance, maybe just an inch. Not transferring weight as you did in prior years will put the bottom of the swing more toward the center than the left center of your stance. Might as well have the ball there!

To compensate for less ability to turn your body, try to "open" your stance slightly. Opening the stance simply means that a line across your toes (for right-handed players) points to the left of the target. It is much easier to turn toward the target on the follow-through when the stance is open.

An adjustment that is not quite as extreme as opening the stance is to flare out your front foot so that it is more than the quarter turn that I mentioned earlier. Many players stand with their feet pointing straight ahead. This restricts the ability to turn the hips toward the target. You can try it yourself: stand perfectly straight and turn toward your target. This flare adjustment will increase your ability to transfer your weight and "get through the ball."

The Waggle

The waggle is the movement you make with the club before you swing. It consists of those two or three mini-swings before you actually swing the club. The waggle sets

The waggle helps you get the feel of the upcoming shot.

the tone for the swing. If you are attempting to play a high, soft shot, the waggle should be slow and soft. If you are attempting to play a low, driving shot, the waggle should be quick and brisk. You should never try to "groove" your waggle; each shot is different and will have a different feel. So, use the waggle as a rehearsal for the particular shot at hand. For the standard shot, the pace of the waggle should be the same as the pace of your regular swing. Remember, the waggle should be a warm-up for the full swing, so its pace should vary according to the situation.

The Golf Swing

While a few billion books have been written about the golf swing, I'd like to take a look at it from a more senior point of view. All players, regardless of age, want to hit the ball consistently and have power. As seniors, we have to rely even more on correct concepts to maintain and

Tom Joyce has been one of the premier players in the Metropolitan PGA. Notice that in his address position his knees are slightly flexed and his arms are hanging comfortably.

Tom starts the swing with a one-piece takeaway; the club and his upper torso turn away together.

possibly even improve our performance. The golf swing is a product of the grip and address position. The proper setup will make it all happen. The golf swing is a chain reaction, and if the address position is correct, all the pieces fit as we begin the swing.

To initiate the backswing, the club and the triangle formed by a line across your shoulders and your arms move together. This is called a "one-piece" takeaway. The reason is simple: you use the big muscles to swing the club. There is a definite connection between the "center" of your body and the handle of the club. As in all athletic endeavors, power and control stem from the center of the body. This is also a common notion in martial arts and dancing.

The club handle should be in front of the body throughout the swing. As you rotate your upper torso, or turn, your wrists begin to hinge, and you continue to rotate the upper body to create a "windup." The upper torso winds up and creates power. The lower body, hips, and knees

Tom is starting to create a good windup on the backswing.

At the top of his backswing, Tom is in balance and has created maximum power.

The downswing is a natural unwinding of the windup.

As Tom swings the club freely at his target, his right forearm crosses over his left forearm.

have turned slightly to accommodate the turning of the center. The lower body acts as a foundation for the swing.

The ability to wind up varies with each individual. A supple golfer may be able to fully turn so that his or her back actually faces the target. At the top of the backswing, a golfer who is less supple may be able to go only half as far. It is important that, no matter how much you turn, the club and body work together.

Many golfers ask, "How long should my swing be? Should the shaft of the club be parallel to the ground at the top of the swing?" The answer is that the swing should be as long as your body and suppleness will allow. If you can wind up only halfway on the backswing, then the length of the backswing will be short, maybe only waist high. If you are blessed with great flexibility, you may be able to wind up a great deal more and the shaft of the club may be parallel to the ground at the top

○ **The momentum of the swinging action of the club carries Tom to the follow-through.**

○ **The perfect finish. Tom's weight is almost 100 percent on his front foot, his "center" is facing the target, and his arms are relaxed.**

of your swing, or even longer. John Daly has incredible windup and distance. At the top of the backswing, you wind up and create power; most of your weight is on the back foot, and your lead arm (the left for right-handed players) is long. At the address position, both arms are comfortably extended. As you start to swing, the lead arm remains long and the rear arm begins to fold. At the top of the swing, the lead arm is fully extended and the rear arm has folded.

On the downswing, the lead arm stays long and the rear arm begins to unfold, releasing power. When you strike the ball, both arms are fully extended. After impact, the lead arm begins to fold, with the elbow pointing down. The rear arm stays extended to the follow-through. The downswing is initiated by a natural "unwinding" of the power created in the backswing. You have developed a spring that wants to release its stored-up energy. This is best done with the foundation of your swing, the lower body, feet, hips, and knees. The front hip initiates the down-swing; weight transfers from the back foot to the front foot. Starting the downswing with your lower body retains the power you created, which translates into clubhead speed and a consistent golf swing. The body continues to rotate. (Those who start with the upper body, and it is a common fault, accelerate the clubhead long before it reaches the ball. A lot of valuable power is lost in the process.)

The club swings freely, and the clubhead is "released"—the right forearm has crossed over the left forearm. At the end of the swing, the follow-through, the center faces the target, weight is on the front foot, and the arms are relaxed.

There are a few other concepts to discuss that will complete the understanding of the golf swing. First, balance is a fundamental in every sport and is crucial to a good golf swing. The great player and teacher George Knudson said it best: "Do nothing at the expense of balance." Truer words have never been said about the golf swing. Without good balance, you have no control of the clubhead. Remember that the club

Tom hitting a driver, front view

weighs about 12 ounces and the ball an ounce and a half, so there is no need to swing so hard that you lose balance. A few balance checkpoints: At the address position, your weight should be evenly distributed, half your weight on the front foot and half on the back foot. Weight should be on the center of your feet, not on the heels or toes. (Remember that you should be able to wiggle your toes in your golf shoes at the address position.) At the top of the backswing, most of your weight (about 80 percent) should be on your back foot. At the follow-through, most of your weight (90 percent) should be on your front foot. Practice balance. Try to hit practice balls with the sole goal of starting and staying in balance for the entire swing. It is one of those can't-miss drills to improve your swing.

Another simple concept that will help is to maintain your height, or levels, throughout the swing. If you're 5'8" at the start of your swing, you should stay 5'8" throughout your swing. Establish that good posture and height at the address position. Create power by winding up on the backswing and unwinding on the downswing, to a complete follow-through.

During the entire swing, there is no up-and-down motion. The motion is rotational and side-to-side as you transfer weight. Any up-and-down motion will be a power leak and will be less consistent.

You may have heard the term "releasing the club." What exactly is that? Simply, if you allow the clubhead to swing freely, good things happen. The toe of the club will point toward the sky about halfway into the follow-through, and the right forearm will cross over the left forearm at that time. This normal process does not take place if you hold on to the handle too tightly, and it's the main cause of the dreaded slice that seems to be such a big part of some golfers' lives. A good practice exercise to understand the correct action of the club is to use a miniswing or "waggle." Swing the club so that the clubhead is about waist high on the backswing and forward swing and look at the position of the clubhead. You can actually stop at the end of the backswing and forward swing. The toe of the club should be pointing up to the sky in both cases. If it is not, soften your grip pressure . . . a lot. And check your grip to make sure you're holding the handle in the fingers of your top hand.

Tempo

Tempo is the speed of the swing. We all have different metabolisms and move at different speeds. We only have to look at Nick Price and Ernie Els to see the dramatic differences that can be found in the pace of the swing. Nick Price has a very quick pace to his swing. Ernie Els has a very smooth and easygoing pace. Both of these great players have good balance and timing, but it would be impossible for one of these players to swing like the other—you have to be true to your nature. Even though the pace is different, their mechanics are almost identical. Both have a "connected swing," with the body and club swinging together. Both are in balance and rhythmic, even though those rhythms are at different speeds.

Following are two illustrative stories about taking a lesson to achieve the correct tempo.

Stewart Maiden was a teacher of the great Bobby Jones. While playing in a tournament, Jones could not seem to find his game and requested a lesson from his mentor. Maiden traveled to the tournament site, saw Jones, and said, "You don't hit the ball on the backswing." Then he walked away. Bobby Jones got the message. There's an old saying in the golf world among the gamblers, "If you have a fast backswing, you need a fat wallet."

The best lesson I ever had was from my old boss Pat Cici, at Cedarbrook Country Club on Long Island. Pat was a wonderful player and teacher. I begged him to watch me hit a few balls on the range and, hopefully, straighten out my game. We went to the range, and I ripped a 7-iron about 165 yards, a little off the mark. He looked right at me, took a breath that showed his frustration, and said in a voice that was a little too loud, "You're swinging too %$#&^* hard." He turned around and walked in. Enough said. I started to tone it down and stay in balance. My scores went way down.

2

Course
Management

Hopefully we become wiser as we get older. This should also ring true of our golf game. Through our experience on the course, we learn what works and what doesn't. We learn which choice will most likely produce good results and which choice will lead to a bad score. These many choices are the steps we take to manage our game. Good players do not get nearly as upset at a poorly executed shot as they do at one that is not properly thought out. A classic example of this is the perfectly hit ball that you are trying to play short of the lake that actually reaches the lake! Good shot, poor result.

Being There

Step one to good course management is to show up at the course well before your tee time. To keep the stress level down, I never rush to make a plane or a tee time. Rushing for both, unnecessarily, raises the blood pressure as well as the stress level. I don't mind missing a plane that much, but I surely don't want my golf affected. Plan how long you'll need once you arrive at the course to comfortably prepare to play, and then give yourself a little extra time, since there always seems to be some unexpected delay, either in traveling to the course or on arrival. You should allow sufficient time to register, put on golf shoes, warm up in the practice area, hit a few putts, and have a bite to eat. A round of golf often will take more than four hours and sometimes five. If you don't have some food (fuel) before you play, the chances are pretty good that you'll run out of energy at the end of the round. I try to arrive at the course at least an hour and a half before my tee time. I think that doing so puts me "one or two up" on the opponent who has rushed to the course with five minutes to spare and whose shoelaces are still untied. I just love it when my opponent shows up and he hasn't had time to tie his shoes.

Let's play three holes together—a par 4, a par 3, and a par 5—and discuss some strategy and learn a few tricks of the trade.

First, let's nail that tee shot. Your #1 metal-wood is the club you usually drive with. It is one of the most important clubs in your bag, if not the most important. You should really like it! Finding the perfect driver may take some time and money, but it is a worthwhile investment in both. The driver sets up the hole. If you drive well, you are in a position to hit the green on the next swing—and make a birdie. If you drive poorly, you are always on the defensive—in the recovery mode. Occasional recovery shots can be thrilling, but one on every hole is impossible . . . and not much fun.

If you have not found a driver that you are comfortable with, use a #3 metal-wood off the tee. It may not produce a dramatic tee shot, but it will probably find the fairway. It is also a good idea to go to the #3 metal-wood if your driver fails you in the middle of the round. Here's a little idea that has worked for me when the driver goes awry midround: I turn to the trusty #3 metal-wood for the remaining tee shots, with a promise to myself that I'll play hard for the rest of the round and then go to the practice area at the end of the day's play and "work it out" with the driver. Sacrificing a few yards off the tee is not going to affect your score too much. Tee shots deep in the jungle will.

Allow for your natural "flight pattern." No one hits the ball perfectly straight (well, there may be a few, but too few to mention). All golfers either hit the ball right to left, which is a draw or hook for right-handed players, or left to right, which is a slice or fade for right-handed players. Having a predictable "shape" to your tee shot is a step toward consistently driving the ball in the fairway. If your natural pattern is right to left, aim down the right center of the fairway. Then, if you hit the ball dead straight, it will be in that right side; if you get the normal draw, the ball will be in the middle of the fairway; and if the ball curves more than normal, it will be in the left side of the fairway. The reverse applies for golfers who play left to right: you should aim down the left side of the fairway and let the ball "work" toward the middle.

Sam Snead was one of the best golfers to ever swing a driver. He hit the ball quite straight. Before each round, he would go to the practice range and make his best swing. He would usually develop a flight pattern with his driver on the range, either slightly right to left or slightly left to right. He would then rely on that pattern and play for it when he was on the course that day. His famous words, "You've got to dance with who you brung," which translates to: if your pattern is right to left, aim right; if your pattern is left to right, aim left.

Next comes teeing it up. Placing a ball on a tee in the teeing ground may seem routine, but actually, there is quite a bit to it! The first question is usually, "How high do I tee the ball?" The answer: About half of the ball should be above the top of the clubface. Many of the deep-faced drivers require extra-long tees so that the ball may be teed high enough for best results. A second question is, "Which side of the tee box do I tee the ball on?" The answer: You should be playing away from trouble, so, if the trouble or out-of-bounds area is on the right side of the fairway, tee up on the right side of the tee box. (A lot of players do the reverse: they get on the wrong side of the tee box and actually aim toward the trouble.)

Another problem is not finding a level place on the tee box. The markers that define the tee box are sometimes set in the wrong place, maybe on a downhill. On many courses, the tee markers are not changed often enough creating unusual wear on the grass, and you may feel as if you're teeing up in a trough. There is a solution to these problems. According to the USGA Rules of Golf, the teeing ground is defined as an imaginary line between the markers that extends directly back two club lengths. So, the teeing ground is not only a line between the markers, but also a rectangle that extends back from those markers about seven feet. Usually, if you tee the ball up behind the markers, you will find a level spot where the quality of the grass is better.

The final step to the act of teeing the ball up is properly lining up the target. Ignore the direction the tee markers or the tees themselves are aimed. Draw an imaginary line from the ball to your target, just as you would in a stroke from the fairway. Often, the tee or the tee markers will not aim directly down the fairway. This can be a fault of construction, a trick by a devious architect, or the tee markers may have been set incorrectly. The maintenance staff, even at the best courses, are not perfect. A maintenance staff member who incorrectly sets the tee markers may be responsible for a lot of tee shots rattling around in the trees.

Okay, we're ready to play. The first hole is par 4, with 355 yards to a slightly uphill green. My drive is right down the middle, about 200 yards down the fairway. The flagstick is in the back third of the green. Now I have to choose the right club and the correct strategy. The distance to the middle of the green is 155 yards. I should add 10 yards to that distance when choosing the correct club because it is an uphill shot. I should add 5 more yards because the flagstick is in the back third of the green. So, I'll play this stroke as if it is 170 yards. My #7 metal-wood will be perfect. The #7 metal-wood also has the advantage of producing the high ball flight needed to hit to the elevated green.

The flagstick is in the back of the green and is tucked in the right corner. What's my strategy? On long approach shots, it is always best to aim at the middle of the green and leave the "pin hunting" to the pros. You will be amazed at how often you hit the ball close to the pin when you just try to aim at the center of the green. I hit a good second shot that finishes a little left, maybe two steps off the green. I have a good lie, but the grass is a little long for me to choose the putter, so I select a 5-iron and use it much like a putter—a little loft to land on the edge of the green and a lot of roll to hopefully get close to the pin. I hit a good shot five feet short and miss the putt: a bogey 5 to start—okay so far.

The second hole is a downhill par 3, measuring 140 yards, and the flagstick is in the front of the green. In my club selection I will consider that the ball will go farther downhill and that the flagstick is forward; therefore, 140 yards will play like 130 yards. If my 140 club is a 6-iron, I should use the 7-iron to compensate for the downhill slope and the flagstick's position in the front of the green. And now a simple tip: Always use a tee when the rules allow. It's about the only time you can get a guaranteed perfect lie. Most teeing grounds get a lot of traffic, and just placing the ball on the grass, without a tee, will most likely produce a poor lie. When teeing the ball up with an iron, a simple guide is that the middle of the clubface should be even with the middle or equator of the ball so the top half of the ball is slightly higher than the clubface. So, I tee off with the 7-iron, but I haven't hit it solid, and it is 10 feet short of the green. The area in front of the green is dry, and the grass is short. One excellent option in this case is to use a putter. In general, the putter is always a good choice if the area through which you're playing has short grass, similar to a green. I gauge the distance and size of the putting stroke perfectly, and the ball finishes inches from the cup. An easy tap-in par.

The third hole is a 485-yard, downhill par 5 with a lake in front of the green. There is an out-of-bounds area down the right side of the fairway, so I tee up on the right side and hit a beautiful tee shot right down the middle, 220 yards. The lake is 80 yards in front of this par-5 green and that leaves 265 yards to the green and 185 yards to the front edge of the lake. I know I can't go for the green, since 265 yards over water is surely too long a carry, so I decide to "lay up" short of the water. Another tip: If you're going to lay up short of a hazard, lay up! By that, I mean do not try to play it cozy and hit the ball just short of the water's edge. Crazy things happen in this game, and just when you're trying to make a nice, smooth swing, the ball rockets off the club—and what you thought was a simple layup shot winds up in the lake! With that in mind, I'll play this second shot with a 6-iron, the club I use for 140 yards, which will leave my ball 125 yards short of the green and definitely not in the water.

A shot of 125 yards over water can be a little scary for all golfers. There's something about an "over the water" shot that takes our focus away from the task at hand and makes us feel as if that small lake is the

Atlantic Ocean! The best way to be successful in this situation, and in similar nerve-racking spots, is to use a two-part strategy: first, define and imagine the stroke you're trying to play, and second, stick to your routine. If your normal routine is to take one practice swing, take two looks at the target and swing: do the same thing here and in other pressure situations. As noted in Chapter 1, when we face a challenging shot, we often stand over the ball longer than we normally would, but more time over the ball only leads to more stress, more tension, and poor results. I hit the 7-iron fairly well but pull it to the left, in the bunker.

I'm now facing a tricky bunker shot. Fortunately, I know the trick: open the stance, lay back the clubface, aim "way" behind the ball (maybe three inches), swing hard, and follow-through. You may not get any style points with this approach, and controlling distance will be difficult, but you will be out of the bunker and on the green. Happily, I get out of the bunker and now have a fast, downhill putt of 20 feet.

Every now and then, we have a putt that appears to be so much downhill that we just know we will hit the ball too hard and way past the hole. There is a method to putting in this situation besides using a short stroke. Try this on fast downhill putts: address the ball far out on the toe of the putter, and grip the handle very softly. When you then make the putting stroke, you can actually feel the putter "give" a little as you make contact. It's the opposite of hitting the putt on the "sweet spot"; it's actually hitting the ball on the "dull spot" of the putter. With that approach, I roll my putt close to the hole for a bogey. A bogey-par-bogey start—not bad.

There are many situations that require good course management and some creative thinking. The rest of this chapter tackles the most common ones.

Uneven Lies

Not infrequently, we play a course that appears to have been designed more for a mountain goat than a normal golfer. Particularly in the mountains, it seems that we never get a level lie, but even relatively flat courses pose these problems. The situations are often subtle, but we still have to allow for them. This is a wonderful opportunity for the senior player to show some true savvy and knowledge of the game. There is a simple way to make the necessary adjustments: first, use common sense, and second, perform a quick experiment.

Common sense can tell us the obvious. For example, if the ball is above my feet, I should shorten up on the handle of the club, so I don't gouge the ground behind the ball. If the ball is below my feet, I should hold the end of the club so that I can reach the ball. So, the first step is to analyze the challenge, think through it, and make the adjustment. The second step is an easy experiment: Take a practice swing near the ball, in a similar lie, and see where the clubhead strikes the turf. That is where you should position the ball. It is as simple as that. If the club-head strikes the turf toward your front foot, place the ball there when you actually play the shot. This system is foolproof.

Golf lore has told us to change how we position the ball on sidehill lies, but that golf lore doesn't take into account that we are not robots. Each golf swing is unique to the player, and we all react differently to these unusual tests. The following sections cover some of the nuances of the different types of uneven lies.

Sidehill Lie, Ball Above Feet

If the ball is above your feet, shorten up on the handle of the club, and then take a practice swing. The clubhead will probably strike the turf in approximately the middle of your stance. Position the ball there. Many players will "pull" the ball slightly from here and should therefore (for right-handed players) aim to the right of the target.

Sidehill Lie, Ball Below Feet

If the ball is below your feet, hold the club at the end so that you can reach the turf when you take the practice swing. The challenge here is to reach the ball, so you should make an extra effort to take a

The sidehill lie, ball above feet

The sidehill lie, ball below feet

small divot after the ball. If the ball is well below your feet, you should move a little closer to the ball than normal, and then flex your knees more than in a natural address position. This situation poses a challenge to balance, so swing smoothly, never trying to overpower the stroke. The ball flight from this situation will vary quite a bit from player to player. Some players will push or slice this shot, while others will hit it perfectly straight. These different patterns are the result of differently shaped swings. The serious golfer should try several practice balls from this lie and see which pattern develops.

Downhill Lie

The downhill lie poses another unique challenge. As we address the ball, the clubhead faces downhill, thereby reducing loft. The 7-iron then may have the loft of a 5-iron. This makes getting loft on the shot more difficult, so our first adjustment is club selection. In the downhill lie, always choose a more lofted club than you would ordinarily play. In a slightly downhill situation, you may choose the 7-iron instead of the 6-iron. In a more severe downhill situation, you may choose the 8- or 9-iron rather than the 6-iron. Learning how to make the best adjustments comes through time and experience, but I hope I've helped you get on the right road and understand the concepts.

Once we've made the club-selection adjustment, the next step is the experimental practice swing. Try the practice swing in the similar lie and see where the clubface strikes the turf. It will always be toward your back foot. The more severe the downhill lie, the farther back the club will hit the turf in the stance. The swing itself is the same as every other stroke in golf, but the feeling should be to swing the clubhead down the hill. Most golfers try to "lift" the ball in this shot rather than allow the loft of the club to get the ball into the air, so we have to make an extra effort to follow the contour of the hill. Good, solid contact will result in a much lower ball flight than we normally would expect. This is simply a product of the clubhead's being turned in, or de-lofted, at address. We just have to play for, and expect, a lower running shot than normal. And remember, a 7-iron from a downhill lie will probably go farther and will achieve the distance more often than a 5- or 6-iron.

The Uphill Lie, Commonly Referred to as the "Launching Pad"

The wonderful thing about an uphill lie is that getting the ball airborne is easy. It seems that even an average swing will send the ball high in the sky. There are some other aspects of this stroke to consider, however. As we take the stance, the clubhead gains some loft—the 6-iron becomes the 7-iron or even the 8-iron if the lie is markedly uphill. So, when choosing the club, consider that the ball will fly higher than normal but not as far. (You may need the 7-iron to travel the normal distance of the 8-iron.) After club selection, we take the experimental practice swing. Normally, the clubhead will strike about the middle of the stance on the uphill lie. That is the correct ball position.

A difficult fundamental to accomplish in this stroke is a normal weight shift. Gravity wants you to stay on the back foot, and if you do that, the clubface will close and you'll hit an exaggerated pull. To counter that pull (and fool gravity a little), try to "walk up the lie" by overemphasizing the follow-through. From this lie, most players hit a slight pull, as the clubface will close somewhat even if they are successful walking up the lie.

Uneven lies are a fun challenge of the game. Remember to use common sense, take an experi-

The downhill lie

The uphill lie

mental practice swing to determine ball position, and keep your balance. Most shots from uneven lies are misplayed because the player lost balance somewhere during the golf swing.

Deep Grass

Probably as common as confronting the uneven lie is ending up in the deep rough—and it can be equally confounding. Long grass has the effect of "closing" the clubface when the ball is struck. It's just physics: as the club enters the hitting area, the neck of the club is slowed down by the grass, and the toe of the club turns in. Since long grass will close the clubface, our first adjustment is to choose a more lofted club than usual. If you are faced with 7-iron distance, for example, choose the 8-iron. The ball will fly a little farther from these lies and will roll more than when hit from the fairway. A ball hit from the long grass is more difficult to control. This type of shot is called a "flyer."

There is also a neat little trick that good players use to play from the long grass: slightly open the face of the club at address—just a degree or two. We know that the long grass will close the clubface somewhat, so starting out with the face slightly open is a good compensation.

Know Your Distances

Here's a seemingly simple question: How far do you hit each club in your bag? Most golfers don't know. An informative exercise is to hit each club in your bag to a well-marked target and get a good feel for the actual value of every club. Normally, there is about a 10-yard difference between irons.

Golfers often base their yardages on the best-case scenario: a 7-iron hit downwind to a firm green once traveled 150 yards, and that becomes the standard. It's a nice dream. The reality is that the true value is probably 135 or 140 yards. As a result, many players do not use a strong enough club and are short of the target after a solidly hit shot. That's why it helps to realistically chart how far you hit the ball with each club. And don't plan for 100 percent solid contact: it happens seldom with any player. If you really hit a 7-iron 140 yards and you're 145 to the flag-stick, the only club you can hit is a 6-iron. A perfectly hit 7-iron will still be short, but a comfortable 6-iron will do the job. Never plan to actually hit the ball perfectly solid and get the maximum distance. Play within yourself.

The one real "fooler" in the distance game is the sand wedge. The sand wedge does not go very far—it's not designed to. You may hit it 60 yards with a good swing. If you swing very hard, it may travel 61 yards. By design, the harder you swing with a sand wedge, the higher the ball goes. It does not go farther, just higher. A three-quarter pitching wedge is much more effective and accurate than a full stroke with a sand wedge.

Bad-Weather Golf

It goes without saying that when the weather gets cool and windy, you should dress in layers. There are wonderful new lightweight garments and jackets that can get you through almost any kind of weather.

The smartest move you can make in cold weather is to "walk." So many golfers ride in a cart regardless of the temperature. It's difficult to move from huddling in a freezing cart to making a good fluid golf swing. Walking will make it feel 10 to 15 degrees warmer than riding in a cart. Your circulation will be better, and you'll have a much better chance of making a good swing. You'll also have a better feel around the greens. So, walk, don't ride, when the temperature goes down. You'll enjoy the game and win a few bucks from your golfing buddies.

Tournament Tips

Following are some tips for playing in a tournament, or if you just want to impress your boss by playing well.

Play a Practice Round

A practice round always helps, but it's particularly important if you're playing in a tournament. Even if you've played the course several times, you should play the course the day before to gauge the speed of the greens and get a general idea of how the course is playing. If you have never played the course, you have to play a practice round to have a fair chance at any competition. There are the obvious features you need to know: you must learn about the lake that is in the middle of the fairway, just over the hill. There are also those subtle points to learn: the speed of the green, the texture of the sand in the bunkers, and the feel of the course. I personally feel that if I don't play a practice round, I haven't done my homework. My competitors have an edge. I don't like that!

Be Prepared

In your golf bag, you should always have the following items: a rain suit, a rain hat, an umbrella, an extra towel, an extra glove, your favorite brand of golf balls (all properly marked), and a few granola bars. In your pocket, you should have several tees and at least a few coins to mark your ball. I use a quarter to mark my ball when it is fairly far from the hole, so I can easily find it, and a dime when the ball is near the hole, so it is less likely to be a distraction to my playing partners. It is sort of embarrassing to always be asking to borrow a tee or borrow a coin, so be prepared.

Arrive Early at the Course

Give yourself plenty of time to relax, eat, and practice, and allow for some type of delay.

Eat

The first-tee jitters can ruin an appetite, but it is essential to have a good light meal before you play. A round of golf may take four-plus hours, you may experience some weather delays, and you will probably warm up before you play. The total time may be five or six hours. The result is a long day, and you simply may run out of gas. Eat well before you play, and carry a few health bars with you.

Don't Drink Caffeinated Coffee or Soda

Coffee might "get you going" too much to play good golf. Try a cup of decaf instead, or at least a combination of regular and decaf. Drink decaffeinated soda if you have to have a soda before you play.

Don't Eat Candy Bars or Chocolate for Quick Energy

The up and down you receive from a sugar blast will not sustain you for long. Golf should be played with an even keel and tranquil mind.

Warm Up

The best way to get the blood flowing and muscles loose is to start at the practice range with a pitching wedge, hitting very short shots. Just try to hit the ball solid. Increase the size of the swing until you are hitting fairly full shots. After you've achieved some feel, try a slightly longer club, such as a 7- or 8-iron. Work on grip pressure and tempo. Next, try a longer club, such as a #7 metal-wood, and then a few tee shots. I try to hit my last warm-up tee shot just as I would on the first hole of the course that I'm about to play. If I plan to hit a high fade off the first tee, then that will be my last tee shot on the range. I'll end the warm-up with a few short wedges to reinforce the feeling of a smooth swing.

Remember that there is a big difference between a practice session and a warm-up session. Practice sessions have a goal to change or

This is a good way to warm up if you can't get to the practice tee before you play.

improve some area of your game. That requires a lot of energy. Warm-up sessions are designed to get you loose and find your confidence. The warm-up should be just that, hitting just enough balls to get a feel for your swing. Hitting too many balls can be counterproductive, actually wearing you out before you play. As a senior, I joke that I have to find that fine line before I play: just enough practice balls to get loose and not so many that I'm worn out.

If you don't have time, or just hate to warm up, try the "lazy man's warm-up." First, put a club behind your back and start turning gently to the right and left. Don't force the big turn right away! Start with quarter turns and work up to full turns. Second, put a doughnut-type weight on your driver and take some slow swings. If you don't have a weight, swing two clubs (this is not as beneficial as the weight, as you will have a different grip). Third, make some swings at a target, trying to have the clubhead brush the grass in the same spot.

Make a Stop at the Practice Green

Nothing positive comes from getting on that first green and having no idea how hard to hit the putt. Having an unnecessary 3-putt on the first green, or just missing the first putt of the day, will start the round on a sour note. A few practice putts will improve your chances of a good start to your round. And some short chips and pitches on the practice green will give you a good feel for how the course is playing on a given day.

Hold the Club with a Light Grip

Tournament and "important round" situations create tension, which normally produces a death grip on the club. Squeezing the handle of the club is counterproductive. Tight grip pressure will reduce flexibility and control. Try to keep a soft and constant grip pressure.

Breathe

When we are in stressful situations, we tend to take short, quick breaths—or to not breathe at all! Make a conscious effort to breathe deeply and slowly. It will do wonders for your nerves.

3

Equipment

To play your best golf, you need clubs that fit you. The clubs should be the right length and weight and have the correct shaft flex. Club fitting should be done on an individual basis, considering all the various characteristics of the golfer. Manufacturers make "standard" clubs, and they do fit many golfers, but it's like a tailor making a 42-regular suit for a man: it sort of fits everyone but needs some adjustments. Many golfers do need some adjustments to their clubs.

Becoming a senior golfer does not necessarily mean you should play with senior clubs. Senior golf clubs, in general, are designed to fit a senior golfer's specifications. They are lighter and longer, the shaft is more flexible, and the handle is larger. While these specifications may fit you, club fitting is based on some absolute facts. These facts don't change when you reach a set number of birthdays. A certain swing speed will require the correct specifications for maximum results.

Now is a good time to mention the value of conditioning and strengthening in maintaining and even improving a strong swing. A thorough conditioning program as discussed in Chapter 5 will keep you strong and will even reverse the trend to lose strength as you age.

The Shaft

The shaft is the most important element in purchasing clubs that fit you. The correct shaft will help you maximize both distance and accuracy. The shaft of the club is a spring; it bends from the force created when you swing. The bending or flexing of the shaft adds speed and power to the clubhead when you strike the ball. If the shaft is too rigid and doesn't flex at all, you will lose power. If the shaft flexes too much, you will lose control. The correct shaft flex for you is a product of swing speed. As we grow older and lose

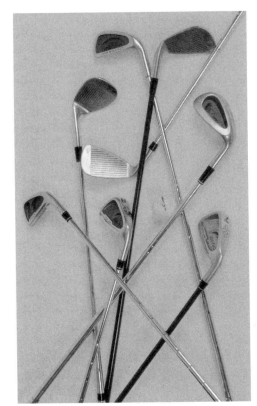

some speed, we can counter by switching to a club that has a more flexible shaft.

My dad had been a very good player at one time, playing to a 5 or 6 handicap. He had a great swing. As years passed and he lost some power and speed, his swing became abrupt and lacked rhythm. He seemed to be working hard and not getting any results. The shaft in his clubs was not flexible enough for his slower swing speed, so he couldn't "feel" the clubhead and make a good swing. We traded his clubs for a set with a more flexible shaft, more spring. His graceful swing returned.

Some shafts for seniors produce less vibration than others when the ball is hit. This is not a minor consideration if you have any arthritis or pain in your hands, or if you like to practice a lot. Graphite shafts, by the nature of the material, have less vibration than steel-shafted clubs. There are also new improvements in steel shafts to reduce vibration when you hit the ball, called the "dampening effect."

The Grip

An often overlooked factor in selecting a new set of clubs is grip, or handle, size. Manufacturers create grip sizes for average hands. Well, many of us do not wear a medium glove, so we'll need a larger or smaller handle. There is a way to measure this yourself. Take your normal grip: if the handle is the correct size, the three fingers on your top hand will just "touch" the fleshy part of your hand. If the handle is too thin, your nails will dig into that part of your hand. If the handle is too thick, your fingers won't quite reach that fleshy part of your hand. Usually, if the handle is too thick, you won't be able to hold the club properly. The handle will be too much in the palm and not enough in the fingers. This will not allow for the normal wrist hinge on the backswing, and there will be no "release" on the downswing. If the handle is too thin, your hands will be too active and you'll probably hit some unnecessary hooks or pulled shots. As a general rule: thick handles equal slices, thin handles equal hooks.

Many seniors have a touch of arthritis or other hand problems. Thick grips can often ease that pain. Several of my students have had arthritic grips put on their clubs. Arthritic grips are much larger. It's wonderful to see those players hit balls pain-free for the first time in years.

The texture of the grip can also make a big difference, and manufacturers offer a wide variety of options. If you have some aches and pains in your hands, ask for the softest grip possible.

Being properly measured for clubs is a science unto itself. A professional club fitter (your local PGA or LPGA pro) is the best source for determining the club specifications that are right for you. Measurements should include grip size, swing speed, and the distance from your fingertips to the floor. Other considerations are swing characteristics and, of course, any preferences you may have.

For people with arthritis, the best club would have a soft, arthritic grip and a graphite or lightweight steel shaft with the dampening effect. It will make a huge difference.

Recommendations

What assortment of clubs should you have in your golf bag? Some golfers like to play irons, and some prefer metal-woods. Which type of clubs we play is a matter of preference. With that in mind, here is a set makeup that I think produces the best results.

Metal-Woods

The metal-woods—you should consider #1, #3, #5, #7 (#9 as an option), and a utility wood. Metal-woods, particularly the #7, #9, and utility woods, are very forgiving. They are easy to hit from the rough and provide plenty of loft to elevated or well-protected greens. Lofted woods in place of long irons will put the percentages in your favor, as they are much easier to play.

Irons

The irons—#5–#9, pitching wedge, sand wedge, and gap wedge—should also be in your bag. Manufacturers have improved irons so that they go farther than they used to go. That's basically good news, except there now is a large difference in the distances you get from a pitching wedge and a sand wedge. A good player using a full swing will hit a pitching wedge about 100 yards and a sand wedge about 50 yards. Remember, the harder you swing with a sand wedge, the higher the ball goes, so it's impossible to gain distance if you muscle it. A gap wedge is designed to be the club for those 50- to 100-yard shots. All golfers have many opportunities to save strokes at that distance.

Lob Wedge

Is a lob wedge a good club to have in the bag? No. Unless you have plenty of time to practice or have a real "feel" for them, stay away from very lofted (60-degree or more) or lob wedges. These clubs were designed for the experts, Tour players who have to hit from deep greenside rough. These are situations that the average golfer never confronts. A very lofted wedge requires a full swing to hit the ball 40 to 50 yards. The miss hits are very penalizing, often sailing way over the green. Golfers will be much more successful using a pitching or even a sand wedge on the 40- to 50-yard shots. It is even difficult to reach the hole on short greenside shots with these lofted wedges. Lob wedges have danger written all over them for most average golfers.

Long-Distance Drivers

Which driver will provide the most distance? There are a few adjustments you can make to your clubs, but, and this is a big "but," there is no substitute for solid contact. We hear a lot about the "trampoline effect" on drivers. This effect is the amount the clubface "gives" and then "springs forward" when it strikes the ball. Manufacturers, the United States Golf Association, and the Royal and Ancient Golf Club have had endless discussions on how much trampoline effect is allowable. As in any trampoline, the maximum bounce is dead center in the trampoline. People jumping on the perimeter of the trampoline barely achieve any lift at all, while the person in the center always goes the highest. The same is true of the trampoline effect on the driver. Golf balls struck in the center of the club go the farthest, so a solid hit is the priority when you're thinking about adjusting your driver in the hope of gaining a few yards. If you are one of those lucky golfers who hits the ball solid most of the time, you can actually add some length to the shaft of the driver to add distance.

All things being equal, a longer driver will produce more clubhead speed and distance. Add one-half inch to the length of the driver, and measure the quality of the contact. You may even want to add another half inch to the club if the quality of the contact is good and you haven't lost any control. An inch may not sound like much, but it's a world of difference in the feel of the club. You never want to overdo this, as the trade-off may be off-center contact (less distance) and some loss of accuracy. As you make the driver longer, you change the balance and feel. The driver will feel heavier, and the shaft will become more flexible. Consult a good club maker if you decide to make any changes to your equipment.

And for the very serious golfer who wants to maximize the latest technology, there are countless combinations of weight, shaft flex, length, and golf balls. The best, most scientific, and most accurate method to finding the optimum driver for you is to be tested by a professional club fitter using a launch-angle monitor. This is a computer that presents all the details of your swing. It describes your clubhead speed, launch angle, spin rate, and distance. Experimenting with a variety of drivers and different brands of golf balls will tell you what the optimum combination is for you.

A less scientific alternative to testing yourself on the launch-angle monitor is to simply experiment on the course. Normally, the club pro has some demo clubs that are available. Sign out a few drivers and find a place on the course where you can hit a few balls with each one. Measure the results for distance and accuracy. This is simple, and it works!

Just purchasing the "newest," "lightest," or "most forgiving" driver may not work for you. To use new technology to its maximum, you have to invest some time and energy and do some research. It will pay off.

Choosing the Optimum Ball

Many golfers ask about the best golf ball for their game. There are more than a hundred types of golf balls on the market. Manufacturers are now making an attempt to simplify their products and reduce that clutter.

The truth is that the USGA has specific requirements for how far a ball can go and how it can perform in general. The tolerances are narrow, and the actual performance will not change too much among types. The serious golfer can experiment on the launch monitor to match the optimum golf ball with the optimum golf club. For those without that time, the best plan is to try a few different brands and determine which ball performs—and feels—the best. There are many types of golf ball construction, giving the balls different spin rates and durability. The basic distinction is that the balls that spin the most, and produce the "fanciest" shots to the green, are the least durable. The balls that are the most durable normally will spin less and are more difficult to "stop" on the green. The major manufactures have developed golf balls for every type of golfer. A little professional advice from your PGA or LPGA professional and some experimentation on your part will give you the best golf ball for your game.

4

The Mental Side

I have had the pleasure of watching many golfers enjoy the sport well into their senior years. My two best examples are my father, John, and Ted Kroll, the champion and gentleman to whom I dedicated this book. They both seemed to love the game as much in their senior years as I imagine they did when they were kids. My father's favorite line when he got older was, "I used to shoot 85; now I hit it 85." My father still thoroughly enjoys a good shot, even though they are less frequent.

Ted Kroll was a true winner. He would negotiate a match until he had it just right. We often played friendly—well, sort of friendly—matches over the many years. Ted was one of the truly great players of all time and naturally would win our match, which meant I bought lunch. (Ted was about 25 years older than I.) As time marched on, Ted reached 60 years of age. He had lost a few yards off his tee shot, so we both thought it would be fair if he played the white tee markers instead of the traditional blue markers, or back tees, while I continued to play the blue markers. Ted once again beat me for lunch. When Ted became 70 years old and was driving the ball a shorter distance still, we again both decided it would be fair if he moved up to the shorter, red tee markers (he couldn't get there fast enough). Once again, lunch was on me. It was my pleasure to watch this champion still be competitive and, of course, to buy him lunch. Both of these gentlemen were positive and competitive despite their age. Golf was still fun for them.

My good friend Dr. Alan Shapiro has said it best in his book *Golf's Mental Hazards*. He describes the correct attitude so well—the attitude I learned from my dad and Ted—that I think it is important to include his insight here:

> They say that oversize woods and cavity back irons are the most forgiving parts of the game. I disagree. Seniors get my vote. Hit a tee shot OB [out of bounds] or chip one over the green, and you can count on an old-timer to ease the pain by telling you that your game's got a lot of promise and that with a little practice and patience you'll be coming around before you know it.
>
> Not all senior adults have developed this kind of tolerant and patient attitude that I have described. There are those who are bitter, who resent the lack of appreciation that today's younger people have for the way things used to be. Of course, their perspective of days gone by is a glorified reconstruction. They recall a time when people had respect for one another, were less wasteful, appreciated the value of hard work and a dollar. It is not my place to present a sociological discussion of people from generations past, but I can state, with some degree of certainty, that the seniors who dwell on the "olden days," who believe that the youth of their day were a cut above the young people of today, who continue to tell the same old "war stories" to anyone who will listen, have not adjusted well to the changes and loss that are a part of the process of growing older.
>
> Tomorrow's life is too late. They say that youth is wasted on the young, and I guess, to some degree, that statement is true. If we could feel the strength and energy of youth and couple it with the wisdom that experience has ingrained in us, it would be no doubt a fantastic life. The only problem is that this cannot happen outside of the fantasy of science fiction or wishful thinking. Youth is perhaps wasted on the young, "must" be wasted on the young, but the real tragedy is when old age is wasted on the old. Rather than take advantage of life experience and wisdom, we look back and dream what might have been, still ignoring—as we did

while busy wasting our youth—the very real fact that there is a today that needs to be lived.

Thank you, Dr. Shapiro.

Mental Toughness

The great players of any age are known for their mental toughness. In fact, when asked by their peers, most professionals claim that mental toughness is the most important ingredient to their dominating an era. The three who come most readily to mind are Ben Hogan, Jack Nicklaus, and Tiger Woods.

A story about Ben Hogan provides a wonderful example of this toughness. Hogan and Claude Harmon were playing together in the Masters and had a chance to win. They reached the treacherous 12th hole, known for its ability to ruin a tournament for any player. Hogan hit first, close to the hole. Harmon followed with a hole in one! They walked to the green. Hogan made his putt for a birdie. When they walked off the green, Ben said to Claude, "Would you believe that's the first time I ever birdied that hole?" Ben Hogan was so into his own game that he had no idea Claude Harmon had just made a hole in one! Now, that's concentration!

I have had the pleasure of watching Jack Nicklaus play up close and personal. I watched him play in the Senior PGA championship at Palm Beach Gardens, Florida. He was on the 16th, a difficult driving hole. The crowd was six or seven deep around the tee. There was a hot dog stand nearby and a beer cart next to it. The crowd was animated. There was a lot of activity. It seemed like Times Square on New Year's Eve and the last place in the world in which you could concentrate on a difficult task. I took a good look at Jack. He was focused. It appeared that, to him, there was no crowd, no hot dog stand, no beer cart, and no confusion. I think he would have looked the same, and had the same routine, if it had been six in the morning and it was just Jack and his caddy. He drove the ball right down the middle.

Tiger is legendary for his tenacity. Even when his swing is not just right, he gets the job done. We've seen it time and again. He's deep in the woods, two strokes out of the lead, and somehow wins the tournament. His record of making consecutive cuts is even more impressive. You would think that the greatest player in the world might like a weekend off every now and then, if he's not near the lead. Not Tiger Woods. It is his nature to be so mentally tough that he always gives it his best, even when he has no chance of winning the tournament.

Mental toughness and attitude are intangible qualities, but I think we can put some definition to the subject. I think there are two ingredients: confidence and staying in the game.

- **Confidence.** We have to believe that we have the ability to play our best, regardless of how the round is going. Golf can be inherently unfair. A golf course has a lot of ups and downs. Golf balls can take some weird and unfair bounces. Mental toughness is accepting those bad breaks and moving on. A bad bounce or a poor shot should not have any effect on the next shot. Eventually the "breaks" even out. We must have the confidence that the next shot will be a good one, and we have the mechanics and swing to hit that good shot.
- **Staying in the game.** We have to realize that all games have an ebb and flow. We may not "have it going" early in the round, but in most cases, we'll start playing better and have a good chance to still record a good score, as long as we don't stop trying. All great players understand and accept that. No player wants to have a poor start to a round, but it does happen. I think the most satisfying rounds of golf are those in which you start poorly but then recover and play those last few holes at your very best and post a good score. Often, the great recovery rounds give your game a momentum that carries over to the next round or rounds.

I had an experience like that years ago. I had a mediocre round going into the Cooperstown Open. I just refused to settle for another mediocre score. I kept positive and tried my best on the last six holes. I posted a good score and had a respectable finish in the tournament. Momentum from that round carried through my golf the rest of the season, and I had the best playing year of my career.

Recovering from Physical Challenges

This is a good time to talk about how we deal with physical problems and illness, and how that can relate to golf. As we age, we are often thrown a few curves, the unexpected serious illness or parts that just wear out. We all wind up with some aches and pains, and some of us have ailments that go way beyond that. Thanks to modern science, many seniors can still enjoy the game after knee or hip replacements. Several of my friends and students have recently undergone these procedures. The lesson I have learned from these folks is that recovery is gradual, and a sensible plan is to get back to your golf game gradually. A good friend, Jim Cocchi, had a hip replacement and eased back into golf: a little putting initially, then a few chip shots, and a week later a few half wedges. Soon he was back to his full game. Golf has become a good barometer of his physical improvement and progress. It can be enjoyed after these procedures and can be the way to continue good health.

And then there are the more serious challenges we sometimes face. I had a brain stem stroke at the end of July 2000, and my good friend Hubert Green had throat cancer the summer of 2003. We are both doing well, but this is a fitting opportunity to touch on the "mental side" of how that event affected me.

I was playing golf with my son, Michael, when I collapsed on the course. I was 54 years old at the time and appeared to be in good health. The paramedics checked me out and released me. My stroke symptoms came and went. For five days, I was in some weird limbo. I'd go to the emergency room only to be sent home as soon as my symptoms went away. Finally, my friend Amy (she thought I'd had a stroke), took me to the hospital and I was admitted. The neurosurgeon diagnosed me immediately, and I had a new home, Bennington Hospital, Bennington, Vermont. I couldn't swallow, eat, or sleep for a month. I came close to going to the "great course in the sky." After a month of wonderful care, I was discharged. (Hubert Green was good enough to call me from Europe to wish me well when he heard about the stroke.) I think it was my very first day home that Amy suggested I hit a few wedges in her front yard. I was some sight: a tube in my neck, a tube in my belly, and a wedge in my hand. I will never forget how heavy that wedge felt—it seemed to weigh 100 pounds—but it worked. Those were the best shots of my life. I knew then that I could make it. I keep improving physically every day.

When Hubert Green was diagnosed with throat cancer, I think it caught us all by surprise. Hubert was never a smoker and was always in good health. He took a great approach: he contacted us all by e-mail and talked about his battle as if it were a golf match against the devil. If you have had the pleasure of watching Hubert in golf competition, you know what type of bulldog he can be. He refuses to lose. And he has the same attitude about this match with the devil.

I think what Hubert and I have both learned is that after a major setback, you improve, but it is oh so slowly, so painfully slowly. I have tried to pass this knowledge along to friends who have gone through similar challenges. It is easy to get depressed, to get down, and to think it will never be the way it was. But, day by day, and inch by inch, strength and coordination do return. It takes a lot of patience and faith. And I promise you, if you have gone through a similar challenge, you'll appreciate a solid golf shot as never before.

Some of us are lucky enough to get a "mulligan" in life. It may be a new hip that allows us to swing pain-free for the first time in years or, as in my case, the "big mulligan" that lets us escape serious physical problems. Golf is a big part of our lives. Take that "mulligan," hit it right down the middle, and enjoy it.

5

Physical Conditioning

The single best opportunity to improve your golf game is to regain strength and flexibility through an exercise program. Stretching, using light weights to increase strength, employing a good cardiovascular program, and getting regular massages will certainly enhance your golf game, not to mention your quality of life.

We all want to be in great shape, or at least we hope to get into better shape. What does it take? According to fitness consultant Larry Feldstein, there are four elements to good physical conditioning that will help your golf game. These are the bases of any well-rounded fitness program: strength, flexibility, cardiovascular training, and (thank goodness) massage.

- **Strength.** By developing muscular strength and power, you will be able to generate increased clubhead speed, which will result in increased distance. A strength-training program that concentrates on the core muscles is advised. It should be done two to three days each week, with one set of 8–15 repetitions per exercise.

- **Flexibility.** Flexibility is the key to developing a full and fluid swing. You can increase your range of motion in your shoulders, trunk, lower back, arms, and hands with five minutes of stretching every day. Make sure you spend a few minutes warming up before you stretch to prevent injury.

- **Cardiovascular conditioning/aerobics.** Cardiovascular conditioning is necessary to keep your energy level up during the round of golf. Aerobics is defined by the 1989 *Oxford English Dictionary* as "physical exercise for producing beneficial changes in the respiratory and circulatory system by activity which requires only a modest increase in oxygen intake." The formula for the activity is 220 minus your age. Once you find that number—which is your target heart rate—you should try to achieve 65 percent to 85 percent of that heart rate for 20 minutes. This level of activity can be accomplished by a brisk walk and should be preceded by a five-minute warm-up and followed by a five-minute cooldown.

  It's important that you enjoy whatever activity you choose so that you'll continue to do it. You can train like a marathoner, or you can use a more senior approach. I have worn out a few treadmills, although not at a high speed. One thing I learned on the treadmill is that by increasing my speed, I improved my performance. Running one day for a half hour at an easy pace and then running the next day for a shorter period at an increased pace is the formula for better performance. If you stay at the same easy pace, you don't ever get to "pump up the volume." Speed it up every other workout, and your performance will improve.

- **Massage.** This is the fun part. To play your best, you should be in the best, most relaxed state possible. Before you play, a massage will loosen muscles, which increases circulation and range of motion. After you play, a massage flushes out lactic acid, which causes sore muscles. Ten good reasons to have a massage:

  - Relieves pain.
  - Increases mobility and flexibility.
  - Alleviates stress.
  - Lowers blood pressure.

- Flushes out toxins.
- Circulates blood and oxygen.
- Aids in healing.
- Stretches and tones muscles.
- Relaxes the body and mind.
- It just feels good!

Stretches

The following stretching regimen, developed by Larry Feldstein, high-lights some simple movements for your shoulders, trunk, lower back, legs, arms, and hands. Before you stretch, make sure you spend a few minutes warming your muscles to prevent injury. These stretches are designed to be done using a golf cart. Footwear should be soft-spike golf shoes, sneakers, or soft-soled shoes.

Depending on your goals, the general formula for the correct number of repetitions is

- **6 to 8** Size, strength, and power
- **8 to 12** Size and leanness
- **12 to 16** Muscular development, endurance, and leanness

The amount of weight to use will vary according to the individual. You should start with the weight that you can comfortably hold to perform a full workout. That amount may be as little as a few pounds for some or more than twenty pounds for others. After you determine the weight and have successfully completed eight workouts, it is time to increase the weight 10 percent.

Calf Stretch (Golf Cart)

Stand facing the cart with the balls of your feet on the step and your heels hanging over the edge; hold on to the rail or top of the cart for support. Lower your heels as far as possible. Hold for 12 seconds.

Calf stretch

Achilles stretch

Achilles Tendon/Shoulders Combination Stretch

Stand with your left foot forward and your right foot behind and to the side. Bend your right knee until you feel the stretch in the back of the leg. Cross your right arm in front of your shoulders and grasp your right wrist with your left hand. Hold for 12 seconds. Switch sides and repeat.

Chest Stretch (Golf Cart)

Grasp the vertical post of the cart with your right hand; keep your arm straight and at shoulder height. Turn your body away until you feel a gentle stretch across your chest. Hold for 12 seconds. Switch arms and repeat.

Biceps Stretch (Golf Cart)

Grasp the vertical post of the cart with your left hand. With your thumb turned up and wrapped around the post, keep

Chest stretch

Biceps stretch

your arm at shoulder height and straight. Turn your body away until you feel a gentle stretch across the biceps. Hold for 12 seconds. Switch arms and repeat.

Back Stretch (Golf Cart)

Face the cart and grasp the vertical post with both hands. Straighten your arms and gently bend from the hips, keeping your back straight toward the cart. When your chest is parallel to the ground, hold the position for 12 seconds.

Male Quad Stretch (Golf Cart)

Grasp the vertical post of the cart with your left hand. Grasp your right ankle with your right hand and gently bring your heel toward your buttocks. Stand tall. Hold the position for 12 seconds. Switch sides and repeat.

Back stretch

Male quad stretch

Female Quad Stretch (Golf Cart)

Grasp the vertical post of the cart with your left hand. Grasp your left ankle with your right hand and gently bring your heel toward your buttocks. Stand tall. Hold the position for 12 seconds. Switch sides and repeat.

Hamstring Stretch (Golf Cart)

Place your left heel on the seat of the cart, with your toes vertical and your knee slightly bent. Bend forward from the hips until you feel the stretch in the back of the leg. Hold for 12 seconds. Switch legs and repeat.

Female quad stretch   **Hamstring stretch**

Hamstring Stretch

Place your right heel on the ground, with your toes pointed up and your knee slightly bent. Bend forward from the hips until you feel the stretch in the back of the leg. Hold for 12 seconds. Switch legs and repeat.

Triceps ("Zipper") Stretch

Raise your right arm and bend your elbow so that your hand goes behind your neck. Using a gentle motion, grasp your right elbow with your left hand and pull it across. Hold for 12 seconds. Switch sides and repeat.

Hamstring stretch #2   **Triceps stretch**

Rotator Cuff ("Hug Yourself") Stretch

Place your left arm across your chest. Hold the arm just above the elbow with your right hand and gently push it toward your chest. Hold for 12 seconds. Switch arms and repeat.

Side Bends (Golf Club)

Stand in the address position, with your feet hip-width apart and a long club resting across your shoulders behind your head. Bend to the right side from your hips, trying to touch your elbow to your hip. Repeat the motion to the left side. Slowly do 12 right-and-left cycles.

Twists (Golf Club)

Stand in the address position, with a long club resting across your shoulders behind your head. Rotate your trunk 90 degrees, with your chest facing away from the target. Then shift your weight to your rear foot and

Rotator cuff stretch

Side bends

Twists

rotate your trunk forward, turning your chest toward the target. Finish with your weight on your front foot and your back heel up, and with your head level and facing the target. Do 12 repetitions slowly and smoothly.

Forearm Stretch

Extend your right arm in front of your body, with the fingers pointing up. Gently pull your right hand back toward your face with your left hand. Hold for 12 seconds. Switch arms and repeat.

Wrist Stretch

Extend your left arm in front of your body, with the fingers pointing down. Gently push your left hand back toward your body with your right hand. Hold for 12 seconds. Switch arms and repeat.

Forearm stretch

Wrist stretch

Forearms (Fists) Stretch

Extend both arms in front of your body at shoulder height. Make two fists and turn your knuckles down toward the ground. Hold for 12 seconds.

Ball Exercises

Larry Feldstein has also developed two series of ball exercises to increase strength. They're both very good. The exercises in this first series are done with a large exercise ball. The benefit to using the exercise ball is that it incorporates balance, the basic ingredient in a good golf swing. Keep your belly button pulled in slightly while doing these exercises.

Forearms stretch

Dumbbell chest press

Dumbbell Chest Press

Lie with your upper back, shoulders, and neck on the ball. Keep your knees bent at a 90-degree angle and your hips parallel to the ground. Hold a dumbbell in each hand. With your hands shoulder-width apart, slowly lower the dumbbells until your upper arms are parallel to the ground, and then slowly press them back to the starting position.

Dumbbell Row

Place your left knee and hand on the ball with your back parallel to the ground. Hold a dumbbell in your right hand and extend your arm. Raise the dumbbell to just under your chest, bringing your elbow upward, and then lower it to the starting position. Complete the set, and then switch sides and repeat.

Dumbbell row

Biceps Curls

Sit on the ball with your back straight. Hold a dumbbell in each hand, with your shoulders relaxed, your elbows at your sides, and your palms facing forward. Curl the dumbbells to the front of your shoulders, and then lower them to the starting position.

Lying Triceps

Lie with your upper back, shoulders, and neck on the ball. Keep your knees bent at a 90-degree angle and your hips parallel to the ground. Hold a dumbbell in each hand and extend your arms above your shoulders. Keeping your upper arms straight, slowly lower the dumbbells toward your ears, and then straighten your arms and return the dumbbells to the starting position.

Biceps curls

Lying triceps

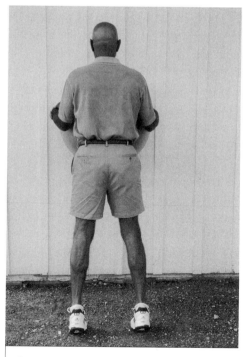

Standing calf raise

Standing Calf Raise

Stand facing a wall, holding the ball at chest level, with your body at a slight angle away from the wall. Slowly rise on your toes, keeping your knees straight. Hold for 2 counts and return to the starting position.

Leg Curls

Lie on your back on the ground, with your calves and feet on the ball. Slowly pull the ball toward your buttocks until it almost touches. Hold for 2 counts, and return to the starting position.

Knee Extension

Lie with your back and hips on the ball. Begin with your knees bent at a 90-degree angle and your hips parallel to the ground. Extend one leg, hold for 2 counts, and return to the starting position. Repeat with the opposite leg.

Leg curls

Knee extension

○ **Crunch**

Crunch

Lie with your lower back and shoulders on the ball. Keep your knees bent at a 90-degree angle and your hips parallel to the ground. Cross your hands behind your head or on your chest and slowly curl your upper body forward, pulling your belly button toward your spine. Hold for 2 counts, and return to the starting position.

Dumbbell Shoulder Press

Sit on the ball with your back straight. Hold a dumbbell in each hand, slightly above shoulder level, with your palms facing forward. Raise your arms and shoulders, moving the dumbbells in line with your ears and over the center of your head. Slowly return to the starting position.

○ **Dumbbell shoulder press**

Front Deltoid Raise

Sit on the ball with your back straight. Hold a dumbbell in each hand with your hands at your sides, palms toward your body, and shoulders relaxed. With your thumbs leading and elbows relaxed, raise the dumbbells to shoulder level. Focus on using the muscles in front of your shoulders. Slowly return to the starting position.

Lateral Deltoid Raise

Sit on the ball with your back straight. Hold a dumbbell in each hand at a 90-degree angle, elbows pointing down, forearms horizontal with your palms facing each other and elbows next to your body. Raise the dumbbells by lifting your elbows, maintaining 90-degree angles, so you feel the lift in the shoulder and your arms are parallel to the ground. Focus on using the muscles on the side of your shoulders. Slowly return to the starting position and relax your shoulders.

Front deltoid raise

○ **Lateral deltoid raise**

Rear Deltoid Raise

Sit on the ball, bent slightly forward from the hips. Hold a dumbbell in each hand with your hands at your sides, palms toward your body, and shoulders relaxed. Raise your bent elbows to the rear and outward, squeezing your shoulder blades together. Slowly return to the starting position and relax your shoulders.

○ **Rear deltoid raise**

Hammer Curls

Sit on the ball with your back straight. Hold a dumbbell in each hand, hands at your sides, palms toward your body, and shoulders relaxed. Keeping your elbows against the sides of your body, and leading with your thumbs, curl the dumbbells to the front of your shoulders. Slowly return to the starting position.

Reverse Wrist Curls

Sit on the ball with your feet shoulder-width apart. Hold a dumbbell in each hand, palms down, and rest your forearms on your legs. Curl the dumbbells up with your wrists, keeping your forearms on your legs. Slowly return to the starting position.

Regular Wrist Curls

Sit on the ball with your feet shoulder-width apart. Hold a dumbbell in each hand, palms up, and rest your forearms on your legs. Curl the dumbbells up with your wrists, keeping your forearms on your legs. Slowly return to the starting position.

Hammer curls

Reverse wrist curls

Regular wrist curls

Machine and Dumbbell Exercises

This series of exercises is for those fortunate enough to have access to a gym. The machines in the gym improve the efficiency of your workout. You'll get the best results from the time you have to spend. Again, keep your belly button pulled in slightly while doing these exercises.

Dumbbell Squat

Stand with your feet hip-width apart, your heels on small free weight plates, and your toes turned out slightly. Hold a dumbbell in each hand, with your arms and shoulders relaxed. Slowly lower your upper body, bending your hips and knees. Stop when your thighs are parallel to the floor. Hold for 2 counts, and smoothly return to the starting position.

○ **Dumbbell squat**

○ **Leg extension**

Leg Extension

Sit at the machine with your ankles behind the pad and your hands at your sides. Raise your feet smoothly until your knees are almost locked but relaxed. Hold for 2 counts, and lower your legs to the starting position.

Leg Curls

Lie facedown on the bench with your knees just off the bench (the point at which the machine rotates) and the footpad on the back of your ankles. Slowly raise your feet and bring the pad as close to your buttocks as possible. Hold for 2 counts and slowly return to the starting position.

Leg curls

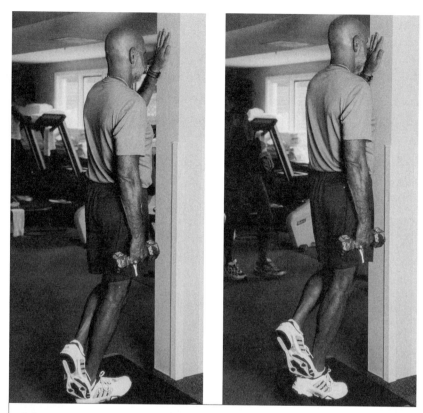

Standing one-leg calf raise

Standing One-Leg Calf Raise

Hold a dumbbell in your right hand with your arm hanging by your side. Place the ball of your right foot on a step, holding on to a post or wall with your left hand for support. Place your left foot behind your right foot, and rise on your toes as high as possible. Hold for 2 counts and return to the starting position. Complete the set and then switch sides and repeat.

Lying Chest Press

Lie on the bench with your back against the pad and your feet flat on the floor. Hold the handles and slowly push them until your arms are fully extended; do not lock your elbows. Exhale as you push your shoulder blades away from your spine. Slowly return to the starting position and inhale.

Lat Pull-Down

Sit on the seat and place your legs under the support bar. Hold the bar with your palms slightly wider than shoulder-width apart and facing forward. Leading with your elbows, and with your hands hooked, pull the bar down until it reaches just below your chin. Pull your shoulder blades toward your spine. Smoothly return the bar to the starting position.

Lying chest press

○ **Lat pull-down**

Seated Cable Row

Sit with your back straight, your feet flat against the support, and your knees relaxed. Hold the handle with both hands, your arms extended and shoulders relaxed. Slowly pull the handle toward the center of your chest with your elbows leading backward. Pull your shoulder blades toward your spine. Slowly return to the starting position.

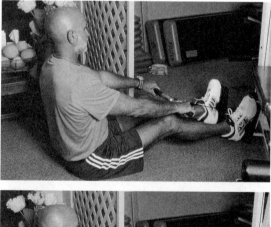

○ **Seated cable row**

Pec Dec

Sit with your back resting against the pad, your feet flat on the floor, and your forearms behind the pads so that your elbows are in line with the center of your chest. Push your forearms toward each other, squeezing your chest muscles. Slowly return to the starting position.

Machine Shoulder Press

Sit in the station with your back against the pad, your feet flat on the floor, and your legs a comfortable distance apart. Hold the handles with your palms facing forward. Slowly push your arms and shoulders toward the ceiling until your arms are fully extended; do not lock your elbows. Slowly return to the starting position.

Incline Biceps Curls

Holding a dumbbell in each hand, lie on the bench with your arms extended at your sides, palms up, and your shoulders relaxed. Keeping your upper arms and elbows close to your body, curl the dumbbells to the front of your shoulders. Slowly return to the starting position.

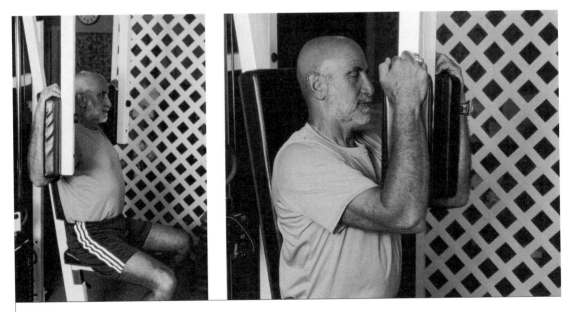

Pec dec

Machine shoulder press

Incline biceps curl

○ **Triceps press-down**

Triceps Press-Down

Stand straight with your hands on the rope or bar in a closed grip. Keeping your upper arms and elbows close to your body, slowly raise the rope or bar to collarbone level. Slowly return to the starting position.

Reverse Curls

Holding a dumbbell in each hand, stand straight with your hands at your sides, knuckles facing up, and your shoulders relaxed. Slowly curl your arms up to the center of your chest, keeping your wrists in line with your forearms. Hold for 2 counts and slowly return to the starting position.

Lower-Back Exercise

Lie facedown on the bench with the top of your hips at the end of the bench and your hands held under the front of the bench. Keep your legs together and your knees slightly flexed. Slowly raise both legs with ankles touching, until your heels are level with your hips. Focus on using your hip and low-back muscles. Hold for 2 counts and slowly return to the starting position.

Reverse curls

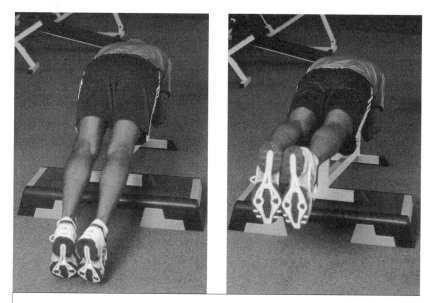

Lower-back exercise

Crunch

Lie on the bench at a slight decline with your feet under the foot support and your hands across your chest. Keep your head and neck in a neutral position and your belly button pulled in slightly. Slowly curl your body until your trunk is almost vertical. Hold for 2 counts and slowly return to the starting position.

Crunch

Abdominal Bicycle

Lie on your back, on the grass or a mat, with your knees at a 90-degree angle. Keep your hands behind your head, without pulling on your neck, and keep your belly button tucked toward your spine. Slowly bring your right elbow toward your left knee as you pull your left knee toward your chest. Switch sides and repeat.

Abdominal bicycle

Physical Conditioning and Golf Performance

I've asked a friend, Dr. Jack Graham, for some insight on how physical conditioning relates to golf performance. According to Dr. Graham, we all have different body types, which affect the balancing act between strength and flexibility. Some of us are muscular but may have little flexibility. Others may show little strength but have great flexibility. Given the choice between these two attributes, flexibility is more important. It increases club speed, which creates distance. The ideal, though, is to have flexibility while maintaining optimal muscle strength.

You can improve flexibility in a variety of ways. If you have the time and inclination, yoga is the best. I think yoga is great. It helped me improve my breathing and posture and gave me the feeling that my muscles and joints had been slowly and beneficially stretched and loosened. The best part about my classes has been the attitude of my instructor. She thoroughly enjoyed the fact that I was giving yoga a try. I wasn't nearly as agile as the "flatbellies" to start out, but I did see gradual improvement. I think yoga will help you cheat the calendar a bit as well as improve your golf. Harvey Penick, arguably one of the most famous teaching pros of the 20th century, said, "I can't imagine a more useful pursuit for a golfer than the study of yoga." Yoga teaches complete and intense concentration of the mind, as well as an artful, healthy stretching of the muscles. It is the perfect regimen for golf. There are videos, DVDs, and books on the subject to fit individual styles and needs. The best book I found is *Yoga for Golfers*, by Katherine Roberts, published by McGraw-Hill. This book relates many of the yoga positions to postures and moves in the golf swing.

For those who don't have time for a full yoga workout, a 5- to 10-minute daily program—such as the one detailed earlier in this chapter—with stretches held for a maximum of 30 seconds, would be a good start.

Your Bones, Strength, and Flexibility

As a senior golfer, you have numerous considerations regarding not only your swing but also your safety while playing the game. A primary consideration is the health of your bones and joints. Old fractures, especially of the hips and hands, can affect grip; fractures of the lower extremities affect your weight distribution, posture, and balance. If you have lower-extremity problems such as arthritic hips or knees, or joint replacements, you may benefit by "toeing out" your left foot at address. This will facilitate an easier weight transfer to the left side and clear the hips more easily for your power into the swing without aggravating a degenerative joint. Along with arthritic changes of the hip and lower back comes inelasticity of the joints. Old injuries, years of poor posture, or congenital defects in bone structure can create a lot of pain. Even the act of bending to pick up the ball can be painful.

A related consideration for today's senior golfers is osteoporosis. As we get on in years, we all have a tendency (men as well as women) to lose bone density by the process of calcium loss. Some individuals will lose calcium more rapidly than others. This condition creates fragile or brittle bones. Care should be taken when walking on steep side hills. Side hills will put a lot of stress on joints, and a misstep can cause injury. A fall can fracture the leg or hip or compress vertebrae. Stepping into a root on the follow-through of a golf swing can buy you a fractured wrist or lower arm and knock you out for the rest of the season. One of the best counters to osteoporosis is weight-bearing exercise. Therefore, walking the golf course is not only enjoyable but also good for bone health. Of course, always take your calcium supplement and get at least 15 minutes of sunshine each day to metabolize vitamin D. Again, walking the course on a fine sunny day—just what the doctor ordered!

A history of surgeries can also take a toll on flexibility—especially when it comes to the golf swing. The problem with a "successful" surgical procedure is that it results in the formation of scar tissue. Typical problems involve the shoulders, elbows, hips, and disks. While tearing of muscles, ligaments, or tendons (be it from trauma or surgical intervention) heals over time, nature plays a dirty trick and replaces that nice elastic tissue with scar tissue. This repair material can restrict range of motion and contribute to adhesions. Obviously, flexibility in the swing can be profoundly affected. Larry Feldstein has suggested appropriate pre- and postround stretching exercises, but don't stop there. Flexibility should be a year-round endeavor. Yoga classes for seniors are extremely popular and are a great way to achieve and maintain joint flexibility.

Strength Versus Flexibility

As mentioned earlier, the goal is to have broad flexibility while maintaining optimal muscle strength. Annika, Tiger, Duval, Garcia, and many other pros are acutely aware of that balance. They are all extremely flexible. However, these young athletes (yes, golf is an athletic endeavor!) are dedicated to weight-lifting programs during their off-season. They are also concerned about their stamina and incorporate a cardio program into their regimens as well.

Strengthening the legs by doing squats, lunges with weights, leg curls, leg extensions, and abduction exercises of the gluteus maximus muscles creates a tremendous power source for your swing. Strengthening the muscles around the spine cannot be emphasized enough. Power in the golf swing comes from the core of the body, the abdomen and lower back. As an example, we can look at how well Fred Couples has done recently after an exercise program that concentrated on strengthening his back. The last areas to strengthen are the upper extremities. Bench presses, deltoid lifts, arm curls and extensions, and squeezing a rubber ball or clay will help you increase clubhead speed. Remember, light weights with lots of reps will do the trick. The concept is to tone your muscles; that means increasing strength without increasing bulk muscle mass.

6

Nutrition

Recently we have become much more aware of what we eat. How we eat affects our performance in golf and any other activity. Physical activity takes energy. To create sufficient energy for activity, we need sufficient fuel. Good nutrition is the basis for properly charging our bodies so we can perform at our very best.

My students, friends, and fellow golfers often talk about the great round they had going, only to fall apart at the end. There was a time when I would have thought their swings had abandoned them, or perhaps faulty course management caused the weak finish. Now the first question I ask is, "What did you eat and when?" I have found that poor eating habits are directly proportional to poor performance, particularly in not being able to finish the round. So many players simply run out of gas.

A long discussion of nutrition needs is beyond the scope of this book and this writer. But with the help of my good friend Dr. Harry Haroutunian, I'd like to present some tried-and-true principles that are well worth addressing.

Average Joe

Let's look at an all-too-familiar scenario for the average golfer. We'll call him Joe. On Saturday evening, he enjoys the rituals of summer with friends: a couple of cocktails in the late afternoon, a nice big steak on the grill with a glass of wine, and then some more wine, dessert, coffee, a nice snifter of cognac, and perhaps a cigar to top off the evening.

Then Joe goes off to bed to toss and turn and actually tries to digest. He must get a few hours of rest before the alarm rings at 5:30. He has a 7:05 tee time and would like to arrive at the course a little early to warm up on the range.

Groggy with low blood sugar and a still high blood-alcohol level, Joe arises and drives to the course, where coffee and Danish await. Joe has miscalculated his time, so he's running late and forced to skip the warm-up. Joe and his friends report to the starter and are off to play.

Fired by the caffeine and sugar, Joe manages a successful start for the first four or five holes, and then the floor falls beneath him. His blood sugar drops, and a voracious hunger announces its arrival. His concentration wanes. His hands sweat and shake, and he notices some tension in his shoulders. Joe's alarms are going off. Joe slices his tee shot into the woods and then reaches into his bag to find a candy bar that's perhaps a season or two old. He devours it despite its proximity to the DEET bug repellent in the lower pouch. And the sugar spike and plummet start once again.

When they get to the 9th hole, a snack bar beckons our boy. (My friend Dr. Harry calls snack bars "the pitfalls of the clubhouse"—so true.) Joe has been able to smell that fat, juicy hamburger since the 7th hole. He cannot resist.

You know the rest. Our droopy hero can barely get out of the cart by the 12th hole to hit his tee shot. The vital oxygen and blood that should be in his muscles to help him perform, and in his head to help him concentrate, are in his stomach to help him work on the burger, the pickle, and the candy bar. He has had no water but recognizes his thirst and waves over the person driving the beverage cart so he can have a nice cold . . . you guessed it, beer. One hundred and ten strokes later, Joe laments his lack of talent for this elusive game just enough to justify a trip to the 19th hole. There, he downs more beer and some salty gold-fish crackers before he has a sleepy ride home to the hammock.

Unfortunately, some of us must plead guilty to having a little "Joe" in us. Joe fizzled like a Roman candle on the Fourth of July. His game went sour for predictable reasons. It almost had to. Insufficient nutrition and hard-to-digest food compound the difficulty of the game and stack the deck against performing at our best. While this may be an extreme example of poor dietary management and its effect on one's game, the fact is that having the right fuel in the tank is a prerequisite to performing well.

Feel Better, Play Better

Control of your blood sugar has short- and long-term health benefits. In the short term, it has positive effects on your energy level, mental activity, ability to concentrate and relax, physical endurance, and hunger. Maintaining the correct blood sugar level combined with proper hydration will give you the best chance for top performance on the course and pretty much anywhere else. In the long term, its effect on overall health is to greatly decrease the chance of developing diabetes and cardiovascular disease.

The following paragraphs offer some simple suggestions to help you feel and play better.

Eat light and avoid excessive alcohol and caffeine the night before your game. This will give you an enormous advantage in the next morning's match. You'll awaken refreshed, feeling good, and not famished. A little stretching, a hot shower, and you're good to go. A cup or two of whole-grain cereal with low-fat milk and sliced fruit or a protein drink will provide sustaining fuel until midmorning.

A low-carb, high-protein energy bar is a great boost for that 5th- or 6th-hole slump (another energy bar is handy on the back nine). If you must eat at the 9th-hole snack bar, try a high-protein, low-carb snack. Salty snacks make no sense. Also avoid any products made with white sugar or white flour. It is best to request whole-grain breads or wraps for your sandwich. A good choice for the correct food source is a light salad that includes shrimp or turkey. And there is nothing wrong with sharing a turkey sandwich with your playing partner to avoid that full feeling.

Remember we are trying to keep the blood sugar in balance—no highs and lows. Variances in blood sugar level can produce side effects that alter breathing, vision, concentration, enthusiasm, and the pure pleasure of the game. For more information about blood sugar, the best source is Dr. Bob Arnot's *Guide to Turning Back the Clock*.

Water is enormously important. Three or four pints per 18 holes is an appropriate amount on a summer day. When you are thirsty, you're already somewhat dehydrated, so don't wait until thirst sets in before you hydrate.

If coffee is a must in your life, try a 50-50 combo of decaf and regular coffee, and limit yourself to one cup of high test or two cups of the combo (that's cup, not travel bucket!). Caffeine may make you perform quickly, but it can also make you shaky and tense. It also gives you a bad attitude. So, be careful.

My good friend Dr. Harry doesn't want to belabor the point about alcohol. We're all trying to have fun on the golf course, that's for sure, but alcohol won't help your game.

Good nutrition and hydration will improve how you feel and how you play. It will also help you get the best of some of the cronies on the course.

7

The Short Game

The short game—chipping, pitching, and other shots around the green—is the place for the senior to really save some strokes. An improved short game can more than make up for a few yards lost off the tee shot. A good understanding of the techniques of the short game and some diligent practice can produce the best golf scores of your life!

That understanding starts with a few basic concepts. First, make all the strokes around the green as simple as possible. You don't have to hit a fancy shot when a utilitarian one will do. Second, imagination is a key to golf, especially in the short game. Picture the shot you're trying to play. Envision the flight, see the ball landing in a certain spot, and then watch it roll along the green toward the cup. The more often and more clearly you can picture the shot before you hit it, the more likely you are to be successful.

Shots from the Apron

Let's begin as if the ball is just a step or two off the green. This first cut of the grass off the green is called the "apron" or "collar." If the grass on the apron is smooth and short, the ball will roll through it much the same way as it would on the green. In this case, your choice of club may be the putter. The putter is always a good option.

If the grass on the apron is not smooth, you may choose to hit a chip shot, which is similar to a putt but is played with an iron. You should use your imagination now to determine what the shot should look like and the correct number iron to use. For one thing, the ball will need very little loft to carry the apron. That means that you can narrow your choice to a middle iron, a #5, #6, or #7. To continue, as you picture this shot, determine where you think the ball should land. Take into account the distance to the pin, the speed of the green, and how much the ball should "break." The spot on which you choose to land the ball should be only a few feet onto the green. Remember you're trying to keep this as simple as possible and you want the ball to loft slightly but roll like a putt. Learning to pick the right spot on which to land a chip shot takes some time and experience. If the greens are slower than normal, or you're into the wind, the spot should be farther onto the green. (Most golfers initially land the ball too far into the green, and it goes sailing past the flagstick.) Use your imagination, pick your spot, and analyze the results.

If you landed the ball in the intended spot and it went too far or too short, let that be a learning experience. The next time, you'll adjust that spot and have better results. Learning this skill takes some time.

There are two correct methods of playing the chip shot. One is to use your normal golf grip and make a very short swing. This will feel natural and much like just a shortened version of your normal swing. The other method is to use your putting grip and use a putting stroke.

The basic difference between the grip for a full shot and that for a putt is that the handle is much more in the palms for a putting stroke. In both of these methods, your feet should be fairly close together, the ball should be in about the same position it would be in if you were putting, and the swing should resemble a long putting stroke.

A good way to get the feel for the chip shot is to "brush the grass." Before you play this stroke, swing the clubhead back and forth so that it just grazes the top of the grass. This sweeping action is desired and will help you allow the loft of the club to carry the ball onto the green. There

○ **Using the full-swing grip on a chip shot**

○ **A good alternative is to use your putting grip on short chip shots.**

should be no wrist action. The swing should have the same pendulum look as the putting stroke. As you learn to sweep the grass, you'll start to trust the loft of the club to produce the loft required. Using this sweeping action with a middle iron will produce very consistent results, and the best benefit is that shots that are not struck perfectly will still be fairly close to the hole.

Pitching

When you aren't quite as close to the green as the apron, you need a different type of shot—the pitch. The pitch shot is played from about 10 yards to 50 yards off the green. The obvious iron to use in this situation is the pitching wedge.

The first concept to understand is how to vary the distance with this club. What do you do to change the distance from 10 yards to 50 yards? The method is simple: adjust the size of the swing—short shot, short

The pitch shot

swing. To help illustrate this, I ask you to bear with me as I present a fairly corny analogy.

Envision yourself standing in the face of a clock, with your head at the 12 o'clock position and your feet at the 6 o'clock position. The club-head will be at exactly 6 o'clock. For very short shots, you swing the clubhead from 5 o'clock to 7 o'clock; for a slightly longer shot, you swing the clubhead from 4 o'clock to 8 o'clock; and for a longer shot still, you swing the clubhead from 3 o'clock to 9 o'clock. I told you it was corny, but it works!

Swing the clubhead evenly, back and forth. Many golfers use too large of a swing in this area and then slow down as the clubhead approaches the ball. That is a recipe for disaster. A backswing that is too short and then abruptly accelerates will produce very different distances, which is also not good. So, the correct swing and rhythm is back and forth evenly. Pitch shots should be hit firmly. Slowing the clubhead down or easing into the ball on this shot will produce a lot of inconsistent and poor results.

There is another step to varying the distance on the pitch shot. That involves the way you hold the handle of the club and the distance you stand from the ball. For the short pitch shot, the 5 o'clock to 7 o'clock swing, shorten up on the handle so that your hands are almost down to the shaft. Place your feet close together and stand fairly close to the ball. (Shortening on the handle and having your feet close together will help you automatically stand closer to the ball, guiding you into the correct position.) Doing this will help you to "think small." It will feel as if a short swing is natural.

The 5 o'clock to 7 o'clock swing with a pitching wedge will produce a 10- to 15-yard shot for most golfers. As you move a little farther away to the 4 o'clock to 8 o'clock swing, you make some similar adjustments. Hold the handle a little longer, so that the hands are about in the middle of the handle. Stand with your feet slightly apart and then stand farther from the ball. Once again, the backswing and downswing are even and rhythmic. The 4 o'clock to 8 o'clock swing will produce a 20- to 30-yard shot for most golfers. For the longer pitch shots, use the 3 o'clock to 9 o'clock swing. The address position adjustments you make on this stroke are to hold the handle a little longer and stand farther from the ball. A swing this size will produce a distance of about 35 to 50 yards.

The distances that these varying swings create change with each player. If you're a serious golfer, it's a good idea to try all three "time slots" with a sand wedge and then with a pitching wedge and record the yardages. You will then have a good idea how far each one of the time slots goes for you. This will help you finely tune the short shots, and even a small improvement in this area will save strokes.

Special Tools for Special Situations

Following are several short-game situations that we always face and some suggestions on how to save strokes when we encounter them. Some of these techniques may appear a little advanced, but being able to call on them is bound to come in handy.

The Texas Wedge

The Texas wedge is what we call a putter when used off the green. It is so named because many Texas courses are windy, flat, and dry. The areas around those greens don't pose any problem, so many players just roll the ball up the fairway to the flagstick. This is a high-percentage choice, just about foolproof. Long before anyone played golf in Texas, the Scottish and British players had the "Texas wedge" perfected. A quick look through a golf history book will show many occasions in which British players are putting from as far as 50 yards off the green! Jack Nicklaus and Lee Trevino both used the Texas wedge on their way to British Open victories, and Tiger Woods and Phil Mickelson will be using it in future British Open victories.

It just takes some imagination. You have to be able to visualize the ball rolling through the thin, dry fairway. If you find yourself in a situation where the ground is firm and the grass is thin and dry, give it a try.

The Flop Shot

Another short-game stroke saver is the flop shot. This shot has a high trajectory and is useful for playing over bunkers, water hazards, or long rough. We normally use this style of shot in the 10- to 30-yard distance range. So often, we have to hit the ball over trouble. If we were to play the standard pitch shot, we'd have to just carry the obstacle and then play for the normal roll. So instead, we use the flop shot. The premise here is that the high flight will easily carry the ball onto the middle of the green. This high arc will land the ball softly on the green with little or no roll. The high arc also eliminates the need of just carrying the bunker or hazard. In effect, we have taken the trouble out of play.

Executing the flop shot begins with selecting the correct club. The sand wedge and lob wedge are good choices for this particular shot. The stance should be slightly open (a line across the toes points to the left of the target), and the ball should be positioned forward in the stance. Grip pressure should be light. A big, slow, relaxed practice swing before you hit the shot will help you gain the "feel" of a soft shot. To play this stroke,

The flop shot: play the ball forward; use a big, slow swing and keep the arms moving.

take a big, slow swing and keep your arms moving. The energy from the swing will loft the ball up. Golfers make mistakes on this stroke by trying to scoop the ball with their hands and wrists. If you can keep the club swinging, good things will happen.

Stroke Savers in the Grass

Now let's say you're in deep grass, with a poor lie around the green. A poor lie is when a ball is lying deep in the grass and you know you can't possibly slide the leading edge of the club under the ball, so you have to make an adjustment. The best club for this shot is the sand wedge, as it has plenty of loft and some extra weight. To dig the ball out of the long grass, apply the same technique as you would for a buried lie in the sand bunker. Square the stance, and position the ball back in the stance (even opposite the back foot). This setup will create a steep downswing, which will force the leading edge of the club down into the turf and below the ball. The loft of the club and downward pressure will "pop" the ball into the air.

A challenge here is that it is difficult to control the distance the ball flies. The ball will also roll quite a bit, so this is a hard shot to get close to the flagstick. If you are faced with this situation, play conservatively and have realistic expectations. Just hitting the ball on the green from the deep grass with a poor lie should make us all happy. Fortunately, you won't get too many shots like this in a season.

We face one of the more difficult shots around the green when the ball is one or two steps off the green, nestled down in the rough. It's not easy to hit the ball cleanly. The clubhead catches the grass before the ball, and you have little control. Usually, we barely move the ball, and so the next time we're faced with a similar situation, we swing harder and the ball goes sailing over the green.

A nifty and fairly new technique for this situation is to use a 3- or 5-wood! It may sound unconventional, but it works. Tiger has popularized this technique, and now it is SOP among professional golfers. The technique is simple: shorten up on the handle of your 3- or 5-wood so it feels like a putter to you. Now brush the grass with the clubhead

A ball nestled down in the grass, just off the green

"Putting" the ball from the light rough

in your practice stroke. Stroke the ball as you would a putt. The bottom of the metal-wood will contact the middle of the ball, and the ball will roll like a putt. This does require some practice and some time to acquire the right "feel" for distance. The key to success with this technique is to swing the clubhead low to the grass and have a good follow-through.

Another situation that occurs every now and then is a ball that finishes just off the green but flush against the longer fairway cut of grass. Again, it is difficult to cleanly hit the ball with the face of a chipping iron. There are two ways to play this shot. The first is to select a sand wedge. Shorten on the handle so that the sand wedge is approximately the length of your putter. Address the ball with the leading edge of the wedge lined up with the middle of the ball. Make a normal putting stroke, with the leading edge of the club contacting the ball right at the equator. The clubhead will not get caught up in the rough; you'll have clean contact, and the ball will roll like a putt. This also takes practice to acquire some "feel" for distance.

A second way to play this shot is with a putter, but you do have to make some adjustments. If you use the standard address position, the putter head will contact grass before it reaches the ball. The adjustment is to play the ball back in the stance. This will create a steep downswing, and the putter head will come down almost directly on top of the ball. The ball will "pop up" for a short distance and then roll like a putt. Once again, this takes some practice, but it will work like a charm once you get a feel for it.

Playing Off Hardpan

Hard ground or hardpan around the green can pose a challenge for the best of golfers. There are two methods to play a ball from this tricky spot. Which one you choose depends upon the path you have to the flagstick.

First, if the path to the flagstick is clear, with no bunkers or long rough, use the chip-and-run shot. Picture the shot you're trying to play, where it will land, and how it will roll up to the green. This will give you a feel for how much swing you should make for this stroke. Play the ball slightly back in your stance, maybe an inch or two to the right of center. This will get your hands slightly ahead of the clubhead. Now make a long putting stroke and sweep the ball off that hard ground. This short chipping stroke should feel like a putt, but there will be a little play or hinging of the wrists.

Sometimes, however, you're faced with one of the most diabolical shots of all, one in which the ball is sitting on hard ground or hardpan and you have to get some loft on the shot to carry a bunker or reach an elevated green. This is a shot for advanced players, but since it's about the only way to hit the ball on to the green, give it a try. Play it like a sand shot. That may seem like an unexpected approach, but it will work. Slightly open the stance, lay the sand wedge back a little, swing through the area behind the ball (just as you would in a sand bunker), and follow through. Adding this shot to your bag will take some practice, but it will sure impress your golf partners!

8

Putting

Senior golfers often lose their ability to putt well. This can be a hard pill to swallow when coupled with a loss of distance. In many cases, the loss of this ability is a product of changes in eyesight and alignment. These problems can be addressed. Some seniors just need a change in putting style. (When we watch the experts in tournaments, there seem to be as many styles as there are players.)

Let's start with a return to some solid putting fundamentals. As in all shots, we have to control both distance and direction. To achieve the proper direction, or "line," we must aim the putter blade properly. Our eyes can play tricks with us over time, and we may become accustomed to aiming the clubface left or right of the line. This happens much more often than you would think. The golfer then "sees" the line incorrectly, misaligns the clubface, and misses the putt—and faults the putting stroke. The real fault often is in the alignment and not in the swinging action of the putter.

Misalignment can become routine and can lead to the dreaded yips. The yips, for those lucky enough not to be familiar with the condition, are characterized by an extremely jerky putting stroke. The player with the yips has no control over distance or direction and will always miss even the shortest putts. Again, misalignment over time will create this unfortunate condition. So, let's get to work on aiming the putter blade properly at the line.

Proper Aim

In order for you to achieve a proper aim, your eyes should be directly over the line of the putt at address. They can be either directly over the ball or slightly behind the ball, but they should always be along the line of the putt. The simple reason for this is that when your eyes are over that line, it is easy for you to visualize the path to the hole. The process is much like that of a marksman shooting a rifle. The marksman lines the sights of the rifle and easily can see the target. The same is true for the golfer. Having your eyes directly over the line makes it easy to line the putter toward the target. Some days, we can easily "see" the line and we putt great. Other days, we just don't have it, and we couldn't putt the ball in the ocean. On the good days, our eyes are over the line of the putt. On poor putting days, our eyes are inside or outside that line. Another benefit of addressing the ball with your eyes directly over the line of the putt is that it gives you a consistent setup every day. Consistent setups breed consistent results.

The best putters have their eyes directly over the line of the putt.

Another step to aiming properly is to line up by using the line painted on the top of the blade (almost all putters have a distinctive line), rather than trying to square the face of the putter to the line. If the blade is misaligned just a degree or two, you'll miss the putt. The line painted on the putter will always be more accurate and easier to use than the blade.

A great little trick to help you line up is to use the lettering on the ball as a guide. Once you have determined the line, mark your ball and then replace it oriented with the letters aimed right down the line. Almost all tour players use this method.

Developing Feel

Okay, you are lined up perfectly. Now how do you control the distance? How long should your putting stroke be? And how hard do you hit the ball?

Getting a "feel" for this aspect of the game takes practice. One way to develop feel is to use your imagination and picture the ball rolling to the hole. As mentioned in Chapter 7, your imagination is a wonderful tool in acquiring feel on the greens, and it's applicable as well throughout the rest of your game. Have you noticed that some golfers appear to be so much better at gauging distance than others? "Feel" is what your eyes see, and what your eyes tell your brain, and what your brain tells your hands. These golfers make a point to take the time to look at the putt and imagine the ball rolling to the hole. Others don't take the time and never really visualize the putt. Tiger Woods is an excellent example of a golfer having 100 percent focus on the task at hand. His eyes look as if they're burning a line in the green!

To help attain more feel for distance, try this: address the ball properly, with your eyes over the line, and then look down that line three times, at the speed you expect the ball to roll. I'd like to repeat that: *look down the line three times at the speed you expect the ball to roll*. Build this exercise into your routine. This method gives you the best chance to use your imagination. It allows good input from your eyes, to your brain, to your hands. That is "feel."

How can you develop a consistent putting stroke? There are so many putting grips, stances, and methods that it's hard to say that one is much better than another. Basically, regardless of grip or stance, the putting stroke should be similar to a pendulum, using arms and shoulders to swing the putter.

In most putting grips, the handle is held in the palms, with the thumbs on the top of the shaft. The tempo of the stroke should be even, back and forth. An even tempo will give you the best chance of controlling distance.

That brings us to the question of how to tell which way the ball will "break" on the green. Greens on a golf course are not perfectly flat like a pool table. They have contours; they tilt and slant. That, of course, influences how the ball rolls. This curving, called how much the ball "breaks" in golf terminology, is a product of the amount of contour and the speed of the green. Fast greens break more than slow greens.

Imagination is useful in determining if, and how much, the putt will break. Position yourself directly behind the putt. Try to picture how the ball will roll and how it will curve. Picture the ball rolling—obviously you will aim to the uphill, or "high," side of the hole. Then picture the ball curving or taking the break toward the hole.

The best putting stokes are pendulum style: the arms and shoulders swing the putter.

Putting Strategies

You should putt confidently and aggressively. A lot of times, golfers try to cozy putts up close to the hole. That is not a bad strategy on long putts, but for distances of less than 10 feet, you should always try to hit the putt with enough speed to easily reach the hole. The ball should have enough speed to roll by the hole one to two feet if it doesn't go in. (Ideally, you should have that aggressive approach with even long putts.)

You gain three main advantages with this aggressive approach:

- You can play less "break" (the ball rolling with more speed will not be as effected by contour of the green).
- Small imperfections on the green will not affect the ball as much.
- You eliminate the chance of leaving the putt short.

Few things in golf are more frustrating than leaving a three-foot putt short of the hole. For an experiment, record how many putts you leave short of the hole in a typical round. I think you'd be surprised by the number. A good goal in a practice round is to have enough speed on every putt to reach the hole. A helpful exercise before a tournament or competition is to "overdo" this aggressive approach somewhat. During the practice round before the tournament, try to hit every putt two or three feet past the hole. At tournament time, you'll be more tentative, just by the nature of the situation, and this exercise will help you at least reach the hole during the tournament.

Long Putts with a Lot of Break

Golfers frequently have to contend with a very long putt on a green with a lot of contour. In these situations, always play a little extra break. If you think the putt will break two feet, then aim two and a half feet up the hill. The reason again is simple: if you play an extra amount of break, the ball will be headed toward the hole as it slows down. If you underplay the amount of break, the ball will be rolling away from the cup as it slows down, and sometimes it will gather speed rolling on the downhill, or "low," side of the hole. The result will be another fairly long putt back up the hill.

Slow Greens

Many factors affect the speed of the green, including the length of the grass and the amount of moisture. Some greens are just slower than others. If you're having trouble adapting to these slow conditions, try separating your grip on the handle of the putter so that there is about an inch between your hands. Without changing the putting stroke or feel, you'll have more power in the stroke.

Downhill Putts

You have a fast downhill putt, and you want to avoid sailing it past the hole. What should you do? There is a way to hit a putt softly. A downhill putt can be particularly difficult if the wind is at your back and it seems certain that no matter how gently you stroke the ball, it will go too far. Here's a little trick to help "soften" the putt: address the ball way out on the toe of the putter, and hold the handle much more softly than normal. Now when you stroke the putt, you will actually feel the putter "give" a little. This is the opposite of the solid hit and will produce a soft, slow putt.

The "Listening Trick"

One of the major causes of missed putts, especially short ones, is anticipating results. Every golfer wants to know if the putt went in. It's human nature. So, in our eagerness to see what happened, we look up too soon. Even great players miss short putts in crucial, pressure situations. We simply anticipate the results before we finish the putting stroke. The head comes up, the shoulders lean toward the hole, the putter blade opens, and we miss the putt as a result. To stay steady when you are stroking a putt, keep your body still, and use a pendulum-type swing with your arms and shoulders. Keep your head steady, in the same position, well after the ball is on its way, until you actually hear the ball go into the hole. If you don't hear that wonderful sound of the ball going into the hole after a few seconds, try to guess how you missed the putt (right or left, long or short) before you eventually look up. This "listening trick" gives you good feedback into alignment and technique. It's a great practice drill and will help break that bad habit of anticipating results.

Alternate Putting Systems

From using the long and belly putters to the claw grip and the cross-handed method, the following sections describe some alternate putting systems that you can put to practice.

The Long Putter

With the long putter, the end of the putter is fixed against your chest. If you're using this system, it's particularly important that your putter be the right length. The top hand helps to anchor the putter while the bottom hand swings it in a pendulum motion. A helpful aid when you're trying this is to point your left elbow (for right-handed players) at the hole. It takes some practice to get the feel for distance, but most players start to putt the ball "on line" immediately.

The Belly Putter

The belly putter is about the same system as the long putter, except the anchoring point is your belly. The top hand helps hold the putter against your belly while the bottom hand swings the putter. And again, make sure that your club is the right length.

The Cross-Handed Method

Both Gary Player and Arnold Palmer have said that if they had one fundamental change to make in their games, they would have started putting cross-handed. That's about as good a recommendation as any system can have. The advantage to the cross-handed method is that there is automatically less of a tendency to use wrist action. The bottom hand just pulls the putter toward the target. Starting the ball on the correct line is fairly easy with this system, though acquiring a feel for distance takes some practice and some time.

The Claw Putting Grip

A popular but unorthodox putting grip that has found success among young players is affectionately referred to as "the claw." The top hand stays the same as the conventional grip, but the bottom-hand grip is quite different. Four fingers lay on top of the handle, pointing at the line of the putt. The thumb slides under the shaft, also pointing at the line. The bottom-hand grip actually looks like a claw. Now just make a normal putting stroke. The bottom hand will feel as if it's just gliding along.

An Attempt at a Cure for the Yips

At the beginning of this chapter, I mentioned a malady called the yips. If you never had the yips and know you never will, you are one of the fortunate few and can feel free to skip the rest of this section.

The yips is a condition whereby the player has no control over the putter head, the line, or distance. This infliction has been the scourge of many great players. In the 1930s, for example, there was a champion player by the name of Ky Lafoon who hit the ball as well as it could be hit. Unfortunately, the yips haunted him. He would get so mad that he would tie his putter to the back bumper of his car and drag it to the next event. Now, that's what I call getting even! Ben Hogan was an excellent putter early in his career. He came as close to perfection in hitting a golf ball as any human ever did. Unfortunately, when his long game approached perfection, he got the yips. A good part of Ben Hogan's putting problems were the result of a loss of eyesight, which was caused by the terrible accident that almost ended his career. There is no telling how low he would have scored had the youthful putting stroke lasted into his later golf.

I believe the cause of the yips is bad mechanics, particularly alignment, over time. Your eyes can play tricks on you. If you think the putter is aligned properly to the target and it's not, you will make a subconscious adjustment. This adjustment will not be smooth, because it must take place in a very short stroke. The quick adjustment combined with an understandable lack of confidence will yield some very unfavorable results.

So, the first step to eliminate the yips is to be correctly aimed at the line of the putt. This is best done with a professional instructor, but a golfing buddy can also be a big help. Note: When you do finally aim properly, it will not look correct to you. Your eyes may have been fooling you for a long time.

After you are comfortable with this new alignment, turn your attention to the stroke itself. There are a few tricks to taming that quick, out-of-control putting stroke. Try closing your left eye (for the right-handed player); that will prevent some anxiety. If that doesn't work, you have to go more extreme: close both eyes and try to make a smooth stroke. And whatever you do, don't say I told you to putt with your eyes closed! They'll take my PGA card away! The yips are the weirdest action I've ever seen in any sport. It is an extreme departure from a smooth swing. Desperate times require desperate measures.

9

The Sand Game
(or "Bunkerphobia")

Sand bunkers are a strategic part of the game. They are positioned to create challenges by protecting greens and narrowing fairways. They are also the part of the golf course that many golfers fear most. For that reason, these golfers will "play away" from a bunker at all costs. If there is a bunker to the left side of the green, they will aim far right, often finding another brand of trouble on that side. "Playing away" from trouble will usually add more strokes and is obviously not the shortest route to the pin.

The sand shot sometimes eludes golfers for their entire careers. To some, it is a mystery how expert players can consistently, and almost magically, hit the ball close to the hole. This skill is really a matter of technique. The best athletes in the world cannot be good bunker players if they have not mastered this technique. For that reason, I've packed this chapter with information on the fundamentals of the sand shot, and I wrap it up with some tricks that are aimed at fairly advanced players.

The Sand Wedge

The first order of business is to have the right golf club: the sand wedge. The sand wedge was designed for greenside bunkers. It was developed by Gene Sarazen, one of the great players of the 1920s. All players at that time had difficulty getting the ball out of the sand. They used a "niblick," a lofted iron with a very thin blade that would cut into the sand. Not a good tool for the job. Sarazen, while taking a flying lesson, thought that it would be helpful if the head of the golf club could glide through sand much the way the wing of a plane glides through the air. He bought all the solder he could find and added more metal to the bottom of his niblick. He thus fashioned the first sand wedge and went on to win the U.S. Open, British Open, PGA, and Masters. His new club quickly became a standard for all golfers to include in their sets.

A few tips on choosing a sand wedge:

- It should have sufficient "bounce" and a large enough flange to slide through the sand.
- It should not be too heavy.
- It should have about the standard 56 degrees of loft. Many wedges are available with lofts of 58, 60, and even 62 degrees. These highly lofted clubs are difficult to play, require a lot of practice, and are particularly troublesome for seniors, as the extra loft makes it harder to reach the pin.

All of this may seem a little too technical, but after the putter and driver, the sand wedge is the most important club in your bag. You need the proper one.

Basic Bunker Shots

There are two basic types of bunker shots. You use one type when the ball is lying cleanly in the bunker and a distinctly different type when you have a buried lie.

Clean Lies

When the ball is lying cleanly in the bunker, you have a "good lie." For this situation, take the following steps.

The sand shot requires a fairly full swing to "splash" both the ball and a divot of sand out of the bunker.

1. Use the normal grip and posture.
2. Open your stance slightly, so that a line across your toes points to the left of the target (to the right for left-handed players).
3. Position the ball slightly forward in the stance. The face of the club should be laid back.
4. Look at an area about one and a half to two inches behind the ball; this is where the clubhead should enter the sand.
5. Take a normal swing. The swing should be about the same size as a three-quarter wedge shot. It is important to use a fairly full swing because you are moving the ball and a cushion of sand out of the bunker. As with all shots, a full follow-through is key. The divot or cushion should be shallow. The greenside bunker shot is more of a "splash" than a "blast" shot. The clubhead should slide through the sand and not dig too deep.

After you have achieved some confidence in the technique, you're ready to learn how to control distance when you play from the fairway. If you have a short shot from the fairway, you shorten down on the handle of the club, stand fairly close to the ball, and use a short swing. For a longer shot from the fairway, you hold the club longer, stand a little farther from the ball, and use a bigger swing. The same is true in the greenside bunker shot. For a close pin, shorten up on the grip; your feet should be close together, and you should be fairly close to the ball. As the bunker shots get longer, hold the club a little longer, widen the stance, stand a little farther from the ball, and use a longer swing. To vary the distance in the greenside bunker, you vary how hard you swing, not how much sand you hit through. (The clubhead should always enter the sand about one and a half to two inches behind the ball.) The length of the follow-through is a good way to gauge the distance of the sand shot: a long follow-through for a long bunker shot, and a short follow-through for a short bunker shot.

Buried Lies

When the ball is in a depression or footprint, or when the ball plugs in the bunker, you've got what is called a "fried egg." These buried lies are handled differently from the clean ones.

○ **The clean lie in the bunker**

○ **The buried lie, or "fried egg"**

To play a buried lie, you square your stance and play the ball off your back foot. This will make the clubface appear closed or hooded. This setup position will ensure a very steep angle when you swing, allowing you to swing the clubhead down below the ball. The very steep angle of the downswing will force the clubhead abruptly down into the sand. The clubhead will go straight down, and you'll just bury it in the sand. There is no follow-through. The loft of the club and the downward pressure of the club will "pop" the ball out of the sand. The clubhead should enter the sand about an inch behind the ball. The ball will not have much spin and will run more than it would from a clean lie.

Variations of Difficulty

There are many difficult greenside bunker shots. Let's discuss three of them: the downhill, the ball buried against the front of the bunker, and the long bunker shot.

The Downhill Bunker Shot

The downhill bunker shot is difficult because if we use the standard setup and stance, we will probably either hit

○ **For the "fried egg," play the ball back in the stance and swing the clubhead directly down into the sand behind the ball.**

the ball too cleanly, sailing it over the green, or hit way behind the ball, leaving it in the bunker.

Here's the best way to play this stroke: address the ball slightly toward the back of your stance, use a square stance (an open stance here is a disaster), swing the club so that the clubhead strikes the sand about an inch behind the ball, and follow-through. Because this is a downhill lie, the sand wedge will lose some loft, so the ball will fly lower than normal and roll a little more. You have to adjust for that. Make a slow, smooth swing. The clubhead should follow the contour of the hill. In other words, allow the loft of the club to throw the ball into the air.

The Ball Buried Against the Front of the Bunker

Often a good approach to the green comes up just a little short and against the front edge of the greenside bunker. The ball rests in the front lip of the bunker. It looks as if we could never lift the ball out and onto the green.

A good solution in this situation: take as well-balanced a stance as you can, and when you swing, try to bury the clubhead in the sand about one inch behind the ball. The downward pressure of the swing and the loft of the wedge will pop the ball over the front edge of the bunker. (Most players try to scoop the ball out of this spot, and then the leading edge of the club hits the middle of the ball, the ball goes nowhere, and they have the chance to do it all over again.) Just trust the club to do the work with this particular shot and you'll have great results.

The Long Greenside Bunker Shot

The long greenside bunker shot has been called one of the most difficult shots in golf. It is a well-deserved reputation because you have to make a full swing and still have the cushion of sand behind the ball. There are two different approaches to the long bunker shot.

Approach number one: use a sand wedge and take the stance you would normally use for this shot. After you think you have the correct distance from the ball, stand back another inch. (You should still try to swing through the area behind the ball and take the area behind the ball and the ball out of the bunker.) Standing just a little farther away will help keep the clubface from digging too deeply into the sand, and will provide a shallower divot. The clubhead will have the best chance of "splashing," not digging, in the sand. This will help provide the necessary distance.

Approach number two to solving the long bunker shot is to use a pitching wedge or 9-iron instead of the sand wedge. These irons have less loft than the sand wedge, will produce a lower ball flight, and will go farther. This does take some homework, as neither club has the flange or bounce of the sand wedge.

You should try both of these approaches to see which one is easier for you.

Fairway Bunkers

Fairway bunkers are those bunkers that are not near the green. They often are positioned on the side of the fairways to narrow the landing area or are strategically placed so you have to carry them from the fairway. There are two aspects to this shot: the management and the execution.

The management involves club selection and planning. The club selection should be very conservative. Choose the club that will most easily loft the ball over the front edge of the bunker. If you think a 5-iron will provide just enough loft to carry the front edge, hit a 6- or 7-iron. You should always add one or two more clubs of loft to have the percentages in your favor. Extra loft will guarantee that even a ball not hit perfectly will get out of the bunker and back in play. Playing this club will also bolster your confidence. If you think a 5-iron may just loft the ball over the front of the bunker, then a 6-iron will surely do the job, and a 7-iron is a certainty. In your mind, you have turned a difficult challenge into an easy one.

Planning is the chess side of golf. If you can reach the green from the fairway bunker, play to the middle of the green. Don't aim at the pin, particularly if it is in a corner of the green. Now is not the time to attempt a miracle shot.

The execution of the shot, simply stated, is trying to hit the ball cleanly, almost "top" the ball. We want to catch the ball first, before any sand. If we do hit the sand before the ball, the same cushion effect we had in the greenside will occur, and there will be no distance to the shot. To hit the ball cleanly, make three adjustments:

- Shorten up on the handle; this makes it more likely that the clubhead will hit the ball before it hits the sand.
- Position the ball back in the stance somewhat, at least an inch; this makes it more likely that the clubhead will contact the ball before the bottom of the swing, thereby hitting the ball before hitting the sand.
- Try to make contact lower on the face of the club than usual, more toward the bottom grooves on the iron. This last adjustment is for the advanced players, but it's good for all to know.

Being a good sand player is the ticket to advancing your game to the next level. Practice in this area will help you drop more strokes than hitting full shots at the range. So, if you are fortunate enough to have practice bunkers available, take advantage of the opportunity. Putting in some time there will really pay off.

10

For Women Only

Senior women golfers experience certain conditions that differ from their male counterparts. I am fortunate to know several female teaching professionals, who have been good enough to share some insights and advice for senior women.

Anyone Can Play

Susan Stafford, owner and director of The Roland Stafford Golf School, thinks that golf is a great avenue for promoting a woman's self-esteem and confidence. If you know the rules and can keep up with the group ahead of you, then you can play with any other golfer. Tiger Woods can play with a grandmother, give her the appropriate handicap, and have quite a match. It is impossible to imagine that in any other sport!

Susan also notes that playing golf is a good way for senior women to stay social. There are many opportunities to join leagues or women's clubs, which enables you to meet new friends and socialize with old friends. Almost every course has a day or two set aside for women's leagues. You can sign up at a local course and enter a whole world of new friends.

Correcting Common Flaws

A good friend of mine, Joan McDonald, was the teaching professional at the prestigious Winged Foot Golf Club for six years and is now the head professional at Morefar Golf Club. Besides being an excellent teacher, Joan is quite a player in her own right. She has qualified for the Women's U.S. Open three times and has won the Vermont Pro-Pro championship, the Maryland Open, and the Metropolitan Match Play Tournament. She has some observations she'd like to pass along.

According to Joan, a common swing flaw with most women in general, senior or not, is that the backswing gets too long. If you find yourself hitting all your clubs the same distance or losing the distance you used to have, this is probably the cause.

There are several reasons why golfers overswing, but the problem usually occurs in the setup. Nine out of 10 times, an improper grip seems to be the error. If the club is not positioned correctly in the left hand (for right-handed players), it will come loose at the top of the swing and flop over. Also, if the grip is wrong, the left wrist can't hinge, which allows the elbow to bend, so the club will go back too far. Women tend to have trouble with this because of their smaller hand size as well as lack of strength in the hands. The club must have the correct grip size in order for the left hand to hold it properly. Check the grips carefully when purchasing or regripping your clubs. Add strengthening exercises for the fingers and wrists to your warm-up and cooldown. As you can see, one little hitch in the grip can lead to a major swing flaw.

Another cause for an overswing is poor posture at address. If there is not enough tilt at the hips, the

Joan McDonald swinging a driver

arms tend to lift off the body, which in turn generates the overswing. It's important that the tilt comes from the hips and not the waist. Your spine should be straight, and your head should be up to ensure a proper shoulder turn, which helps load the weight on the right side. This is the power source in the downswing.

The problem with the club's swinging back too far is that it doesn't allow for proper weight shift. The weight usually stays on the left foot going back and falls to the right foot coming through. This is what's known as a reverse weight shift. When this happens, all power in the swing is lost.

Balance is a real key for senior women. Many senior women try to keep up with younger players or try to achieve the distances they had years ago. The first casualty of forcing the swing is balance. Practice with a comfortable club, such as an 8-iron or a 7-wood. You should practice hitting smooth shots, finishing in balance and facing the target. Swing within your own capabilities; don't force it. Make the swing as smooth as possible, and your distance will return.

The Big Picture

Susanne Newell is a teaching professional at The Golf School. Susanne offers some guidelines in five areas important for senior women.

Sue Newell

- **Nourishment.** Most senior women don't eat enough food before they play. (A lot of male golfers have the same problem.) Many are diet conscious and just don't have the fuel to finish the round of golf. Eating a light, easy-to-digest meal just before play is the best solution. Having a granola or power bar along the way will provide the energy for the four-plus hours it takes to play a round of golf.
- **Equipment.** Trade in the midirons for lofted metal-woods. Use #7, #9, or #11 metal-woods instead of the middle irons; they're lighter, easier to swing,

and easier to get in the air. You'll find a wide range of hybrid clubs on the market. Experiment with those; they are very friendly.

A club to avoid or to use sparingly is a lob or highly lofted wedge. These clubs are not designed for recreational players and are particularly difficult for senior women. They require a lot of clubhead speed to hit the ball a short distance. Leave the lofted wedges to Tiger and Vijay, and just stick with the standard sand wedge for sand bunkers and highly lofted shots around the green.

- **Strength.** This may seem like an unlikely subject for senior women, but there is a direct relationship between hand strength and clubhead speed. Small hand exercisers, used on a regular basis, will do wonders for distance off the tee and the ability to swing through some deep grass. Light exercise programs are always beneficial to your game. Look at Annika Sorenstam—she's the best female golfer in the world. Part of the reason is her strength.

- **Practice.** Identify the weak areas of your game, get some good instruction, and practice. The part of the game most overlooked is putting. It's amazing how many lessons are given on the tee shots and how few are given on chipping and putting, where the real scoring takes place.

- **Inspiration.** Golf provides a wonderful opportunity to connect with friends and family. Recently I met with Libby Smith and Sue Horton, who play on the Futures Tour. They were giving a kids' clinic in Manchester, Vermont. Both relayed stories of how their grandmothers got them started in golf. They both had warm and inspiring memories of those days. Make the most of the opportunities that golf presents to connect with children and grandchildren.

11

The Myths of Golf

There is no shortage of information in the game of golf. The golf ball just sits there, waiting to be hit. We receive plenty of advice from friends on how to go about it. Some of this advice is good. Some is not. Over time, the misinformation we collect can become the foundation for how we swing the club. I call this incorrect input from well-meaning friends the "myths of golf." If you haven't received any of this wrongheaded advice, you're very lucky. This chapter is dedicated to a discussion of the most egregious myths in an attempt to "deprogram" those golfers who have been trying to create the wrong motion in their swings for a long time.

Keep Your Head Down

"Keep your head down" is the classic golf myth. Nearly everyone has heard it repeated. It is correct to look at the ball during the swing. You see the ball with your eyes—but you don't have to bury your head in your chest to use your eyes. Lowering your head at address will wreck good posture and not allow room for your shoulders to rotate.

Your head should be only slightly tilted down so that you can see the ball, not at all buried in your chest. If you try to keep your head down, you will unnaturally lose some height at the address position. You will lose power and consistency. The irony of this poor advice is that, if you take it, you actually have to rise during the swing to make room for your arms to extend. This rising motion has nothing to do with golf: it's your instincts! Your brain won't let you break your arms, so your body rises. This is like removing your hands from a hot stove, an instinct for self-preservation. The more you try to keep your head down, the more height you lose during the swing. It follows then that the more you try to keep your head down, the more you actually have to rise to make room to swing in order to keep from gouging the turf behind the ball. You may feel yourself rising and want to correct it by keeping your head down even more. This only compounds the problem. The motion in your swing will become very up-and-down. It should not be. In a good swing, the motion should be rotational and side-to-side.

The correction for this myth is to establish good posture: head up, hips slightly back, and weight evenly distributed. Slightly tilt your head so that you can see the ball. Maintain your height during the swing.

Keep Your Left Arm Straight

In a good golf swing, the left arm (for right-handed golfers) gets "long" as you start the swing. At the top of the backswing, it is fully extended. This is the result of the force created by the swinging action of the club. It is natural. Unfortunately, this correct action can be incorrectly analyzed. It can appear that the left arm is rigid. It is actually quite the contrary. The left arm should be extended but supple. Any attempt to keep the left arm stiff will create tension either in the address position or during the swing. This will slow clubhead speed and reduce distance. It will also lessen the natural swinging action of the club, limiting the chance of the club's returning squarely to the ball.

The correction for this myth is to stay loose and supple at address and during the swing. At the address position, both arms are naturally extended, tension free. During the backswing, the left arm stays "long" while the right arm begins to fold. The left arm stays extended to the top of the backswing; at impact, both arms are extended. After impact, the left arm begins to fold. These are all natural actions and will occur as long as you stay supple.

Pull Down with Your Left Hand

This bit of advice can really be trouble. If you actually do pull down with your left hand, it will be almost impossible to have the clubface squarely strike the ball. Pulling down with your left hand will restrict the normal hand action, the "unhinging" of the wrists. The face of the club will be decidedly open, which will result in a push or slice. An open clubface will also reduce power.

The correction here is to swing the club naturally with both hands. Golf is a two-handed game. The hands work together as a unit. The normal swinging of the club with equal pressure from each hand will square the clubface at impact.

Many other misconceptions stymie the game of golf. The best way to improve your game is to learn the fundamentals and stick to them.

12

Practice Drills and Training Aids

Practice should be productive and fun. To make it productive, first analyze the areas of your game that need the most improvement. Quantify how you play: How often do your drives find the fairway? How often do your iron shots hit the green? How many putts do you use in a round? Once you define the area of your game that is the weakest, dedicate yourself to improvement. If, through practice, the weakest part of your game were to become the strongest, your scores would dramatically improve.

All practice should have a goal. That goal may be to hit more fairways off the tee or to make a higher percentage of 10-foot putts. It is a good idea to have one goal per session. For instance, you may want to spend one entire session working on weight transfer. Your goal would be simple: hit a bucket of balls finishing the swing in balance, with all your weight on your forward foot and your chest facing the target. Having a single goal per session will promote a positive result. To get the most from practice sessions, use a notepad to chart your progress and keep track of swing changes you have made. This will prevent you from following the wrong path and will give you valuable feedback.

You can make practice fun by creating "games." Practice with a friend and organize some competitions. A contest to determine who can make the most putts or hit the most fairways can keep practice light but still focused. This type of practice provides competition while helping you identify strengths and weaknesses.

We practice to improve both our score and our enjoyment. This requires the abilities to change and, most important, to think. All of that takes some energy. Practicing when you're tired is often counterproductive. Limit your practice sessions to times when you can be strong mentally and physically. Many practice sessions do not produce the results they should because the player hit too many practice balls, got tired, and fell back into bad habits. Often, we make a minor change and it works, so then we just keep banging range balls until we get tired, and the old bad habits return. There is a classic story about Jack Nicklaus. He hadn't played well one day, and after the round, he had an idea for a correction to get him back on track. He went to the range and worked it out. That session required hitting a grand total of 17 practice balls. A spectator was amazed to see Jack leave the range after so few practice balls and asked him why he didn't stay longer. Jack responded that he had accomplished his mission. He knew that the correction was made, it didn't need more work, and any additional swings would not be productive. Smart guy, that Jack Nicklaus.

Instruction and information combined with intelligent practice are the ingredients to a better golf game. There is really no substitute for a good professional instructor to keep you on the right track. Minor mistakes in setup or alignment can frequently be detected by a good coach. The trained eye can save you countless hours of frustration. And, of course, almost nothing is worse than practicing the movements in the swing and actually "grooving" a bad swing.

Changes in golf do not come easy, and to effectively change your swing, you may have to use practice drills to totally change the "feel." These changes in feel have to be dramatic in order for them to transfer to the swing you use on the course. They say, "The longest walk in golf is from the practice tee to the first tee." How well so many of us know that. The following drills and training aids are designed to make that walk shorter and more enjoyable.

Practice Drills for the Long Game

Practice drills for the long game are motions we make in a practice area with the goal of improving the swing we take to the golf course. These specific drills are designed to correct a swing flaw or to generally improve technique.

The Toe-Up, Toe-Up Drill

When we have trouble with long shots, we often go to the range and try to find the correction by hitting full shots. A better way to correct the problem is to use a miniswing or half swing instead. Swing the club waist high to waist high. To get a clear picture of this drill imagine the shaft of the club as a leg and the innermost part of the clubhead to be the heel and the outermost part of the clubhead to be the toe. If you're doing it properly, the toe of the club should point to the sky on the backswing, and the toe of the club should point to the sky on the waist-high follow-through. A normal weight transfer will allow you to release your back foot so that your back heel is off the ground and you are balancing on your front foot. If you see that the toe of the club is not up on the backswing and follow-through, look for corrections, starting with the grip and then the alignment.

This is a nifty drill to get back to the basics of the swing. It is a lot easier to correct a swing flaw with a short swing than with a full swing.

The Split-Grip Drill

This drill is particularly advantageous for players who have trouble with the dreaded slice. With this one, you can use any club in the bag. After you establish your normal grip, slide your bottom hand down the handle so that you have about a three-inch gap between your hands. When you separate your hands, the bottom hand normally will become a little more aggressive and you will be able to feel the "release" of the club. The release is the natural result of the force created by the swinging action of the club. Players often do not allow that action to happen because their grip is too tight or they have established an incorrect swing pattern. As with all shots, grip pressure should be light. By using the split-grip drill, you will more easily be able to square the clubhead to the ball and the target.

The Feet-Together Drill

A super drill to get the feel of the swing is to practice with your feet together. It teaches a pure swinging action: if you try to force your swing in any way, you'll lose your balance! When you practice with your feet together, you have to rely solely on the swinging action of the club. It's amazing how often you will hit the ball solid with this swing. With your feet together, you will have to rely on rhythm and balance. Any attempt to muscle the swing will simply not work. You'll fall over!

For this drill, choose a friendly club, maybe a 7- or 8-iron. Make a few half swings, about waist high to waist high. Next, increase the size of the swing to a three-quarter swing. Then make some full swings. You may feel restricted at first because your feet are together, but you'll feel the clubhead swinging. You should then try a #5 or #7 metal-wood. The pure swinging action of this drill allows you to feel as if you're swinging the club with your body. A narrow stance makes it easy for the body to turn, and your footwork will become more natural. Many seniors dig in too hard. A loss of distance over time may prompt the "dig in" response to re-create some old feeling of power. The feet-together drill will keep you light on your feet, enable you to turn, and help you get the most from your swing.

The Baseball Drill

Most players slice—seniors, juniors, men, and women. It's the chronic problem for the recreational golfer. A slice, or an extreme left-to-right ball flight (for a right-handed player), is especially bad for seniors, as a slice will rob you of some distance. A draw, or right-to-left flight, will produce the most distance. That's what we're trying to achieve.

Most golfers slice the ball because their grip is too tight and won't allow the normal rotation of the clubhead. The clubface will be "open" when it reaches the ball, and they'll hit the ball to the right. The baseball drill is designed to help you feel that normal rotation. To get the feel for the proper rotation, hold the club about waist high, and swing it back waist high. You'll feel the proper wrist hinge. At the end of the baseball backswing, the face of the club should point to the sky. Now swing it forward, just like a baseball player. If you do this correctly, you'll feel the head of the club (bat) snap at the ball. As noted earlier, this is called the release in the golf swing. This is natural. As you finish your "baseball swing," your right forearm will cross over your left forearm. At the end of your swing, the clubface will finish downward. That's your golf swing. You just have to add good golf posture to this drill to change the shape or plane of the swing so you can reach the ground.

The Step-Through Drill

So many players have difficulty properly transferring their weight. How many golfers do we actually ever see finish their swings in balance? Very few. The step-through drill can help cure the tendency to hit the ball with weight on the back foot, sacrificing both distance and accuracy. We've all seen Gary Player hit full shots. At the end of his follow-through, Gary takes a step toward his target. This move guarantees proper weight transfer. Try it yourself on the practice tee.

The Preset Drill

The preset drill is particularly useful when you're having trouble with your takeaway. Take the normal address position and then slowly swing the club waist high so that the toe of the club is pointing to the sky. Hold that position for 3 counts, and then turn your shoulders to complete the backswing. This move will automatically swing the club into the correct position at the top of the swing.

Jay's Emergency Drill

Five years ago, my brother, Bill, paid me a visit. He was scheduled to play in an outing with some important business associates. Bill has hardly played any golf, and he hadn't played a single round in years. My challenge was to figure out a way for my brother, an absolutely great guy, to create a golf game in one day. So, we went to work.

I had Bill hit some short wedges, swinging the head of the club waist high to waist high. It's a simple shot. He hit some good ones and developed some confidence. We practiced this for about 15 minutes. Then I tricked him. I traded the wedge for an 8-iron and had him make the same short, waist-high-to-waist-high swing. Because the 8-iron is a little longer than the wedge, his swing also became a little longer. He hit some good shots with the 8-iron. I then asked Bill to go back to the wedge, again getting the good feel of that waist-high-to-waist-high swing. I tricked him again: this time I gave him a #5 metal-wood and asked him to use the same waist-high swing. He hit the #5 metal-wood beautifully. And my brother became a golfer.

The drill is simple: hit some short wedges, get a good feel, and then make the same short swing using an 8-iron and then using a friendly metal-wood. Alternate back and forth, always going back to the short wedge to get a good feel.

The story of the evolution of this drill has a happy ending. Bill attended the business outing, went through our routine on the practice tee, and played very well. He actually shot 48 for nine holes. Not too shabby for someone who barely plays!

Drills for the Short Game

Short game drills are designed to give you more "feel" around the greens, improve your technique, and help you gain confidence.

The Sand Drill

The sand drill is a surefire way to improve greenside bunker play. It helps you fully understand the concepts in bunker play. This is just a practice drill, now—if you try it during a round of golf, you'll incur a bunch of penalty strokes.

In the practice bunker, draw a four-inch circle in the sand, and address the circle as if the ball were in the middle. Swing through the circle so that you splash all of the sand (in the four-inch circle) out of the bunker. You're throwing a divot of sand from the bunker onto the green. After you do this a few times, put a ball in the center of the circle. Once again, swing through the circle and try to splash the sand and the ball onto the green. The head of the sand wedge should enter the sand about an inch and a half behind the ball and then follow through so that the entire divot is splashed out of the bunker.

After you have achieved some confidence with this drill, you can start to acquire a feel for distance. A short, easy swing with a little splash will produce a short distance. A long, more aggressive swing with more splash will throw the ball farther onto the green.

The Coin Drill for Putting

The coin drill is a top choice for improving putting alignment. It is especially appropriate if you are having trouble "seeing" the line. For this drill, choose a flat, fairly short putt (about 10 feet) on the practice green. Line up the putt from behind, and place a coin directly on that line halfway between your ball and the hole. Now address the ball, look down the line of the putt, and see if the coin appears to move. If it does, your perception is off and your eyes are playing tricks on you. Practice lining the putter blade up to the coin and then rolling the ball over the coin, toward the hole. Soon you will see improvement in lining up and focusing on the target.

The No-Peek Drill

The no-peek drill is a useful putting, chipping, and pitching drill. Short shots are often misplayed because we are looking for results before we actually finish the stroke or short swing. For this drill, keep your head still when you hit the ball. If you're putting, keep your head still until you hear the ball fall into the cup. After a few seconds you may not hear that wonderful expected sound. If you don't, guess how you might have missed the putt, right or left/long or short, and then look up to see if you were correct. If you're chipping or pitching, wait until you hear the ball land on the green before you look up to check out the results. Keeping your head steady will ensure that you have successfully completed the stroke. And remember: no peeking!

A prime example of this discipline in action was witnessed in the 2004 Masters. Phil Mickelson had a tricky 25-foot downhill putt to win the tournament. One can only imagine how tight Phil's nerves must have been. Yet, when he stroked the putt, he kept his head still almost until the ball reached the hole. He was not going to allow his anxiety to check out the results interfere with a good putting stroke.

Teaching Aids

Making changes and improvements in your golf game is not easy. We get used to a certain feel or swing. Even if that swing is not correct, it is familiar. To implement a small change, you have to totally change how the motion feels. A typical example is trying to shorten a swing. They'll swear they are only swinging the club to their waist, and yet the real change may be to shorten the swing only an inch or two. A change in a golf swing must feel dramatically different to affect any change at all. The saying "You can't teach an old dog new tricks" has some truth in it. It's difficult to make changes.

Teaching aids can be very beneficial in effecting those totally different swings. They also help use time efficiently. We are all pressed for time and often have limited opportunity to practice. Teaching aids help you maximize the value of your practice. In addition, they give you more of a sense of purpose and focus. Using a teaching aid for an hour will help you isolate the area you are trying to improve. This focused practice is a lot more productive than just banging out a bucket of practice balls.

Video/DVD

An often overlooked teaching aid is the video or DVD camera. There is nothing better than seeing what your swing really looks like. Countless times, students of mine have self-corrected their swings after we've viewed them. The normal reaction to seeing oneself on tape is, "I can't be that bad—that awkward." We all know what a great golf swing looks like from watching Annika Sorenstam or Tiger Woods in tournaments on TV. We know we should swing somewhat, or sort of, like them. Seeing a tape of your swing, comparing it with a great swing, and then trying to copy that swing (to whatever degree possible) is the best way to make major improvements. If you have the chance, videotape yourself right on the golf course. It's best to see what your golf game looks like in the "heat of battle." We all know how we can be fooled on the practice tee.

The video camera is a huge help in the short game, too. This is obviously where most of the strokes are lost or saved. View your pitch and chip shots. The short chip shot should look a lot like a putting stroke. The pitch shot swing should be a larger swing than the chip shot, and there should be some hinging of the wrists. As the distance increases, the size of the swing should increase. Remember that the swing should be even on both sides. The length of the backswing should match the length of the follow-through.

Video can be most helpful on the putting green! Between one-third and one-half of our strokes in a round are on the putting green. It is the one area that can most dramatically affect our score. Viewing and reviewing your putting stroke can give you feedback on how you stroke the putt and, most important, how you aim. As I mentioned in the chapter on putting, your eyes can really play tricks on you. Viewing your putting routine will show you if you are lined up properly. Proper alignment is mandatory for excellent putting.

The Medicus

Another good teaching aid is a club called the Medicus. It is a 5-iron with a hinge in the middle of the shaft. If you make a perfect swinging motion, the force you create will prevent the hinge from bending, and the shaft will appear straight and normal. If you snatch the club back quickly, with your hands only, or start the club down too early, the hinge in the shaft will bend, indicating a flaw in the swing. Practice with the Medicus until you can make a full swing without bending the hinge. Once you get confident with this teaching aid, you can actually hit some practice balls with it!

The Weighted Driver

The oldest teaching aid, and a very good one, is the heavy or weighted driver. You can either weight an old driver or put on a weight especially

The Medicus is a training aid that will help with tempo and swinging the club on the right path.

designed for the purpose (such as a doughnut). The weighted club gives you a feel for the swing while strengthening your golf muscles. Five or ten minutes of a slow, smooth swing each day will add yards to tee shots.

The Impact Bag

The impact bag is a heavy bag filled with sand or rags. It can help you improve both your impact position and your ability to hit the ball. Set up as you normally would, and substitute the impact bag for the ball. Take a normal swing, allowing the clubhead to strike the impact bag. You will "feel" all the qualities of a good swing. Because there is no ball, you will swing freely, as you are not concerned with the result. This drill will strengthen your arms and hands and will create a swing with greater freedom. It will encourage you to transfer your weight to your front foot on the downswing. If you can carry that feeling to the golf course, you will hit the ball farther and more solidly.

○ **The movements of tossing a ball will help you get the feel for the swing.**

Tossing a Ball

The simplest training aid to recover the feel of the swing is to toss a large ball, a soccer ball or, ideally, a medicine ball, because it has sufficient weight. Stand in a good athletic position and hold the ball waist high with both hands. Then toss it! The action of tossing a ball is similar to swinging a club. As you toss the ball back and forth, you'll feel a good weight transfer. It's so natural. Just the way a good golf swing should feel.

The Pelz Putting Track

A recommended training aid for putting is the Pelz Putting Track. It helps you see the line of the putt as well as learn what size putting stroke you need for different distances. As I mentioned in Chapter 8, alignment is crucial to a smooth putting stroke. The Pelz Putting Track will be a big help in achieving proper alignment.

⊸ The Pelz Putting Track

The SwingWave

The SwingWave is a half club with a small container on the end that can hold varying amounts of water. It's a neat gadget for giving you the feel of the swing. It can also be used as a strengthening tool. You vary the amount of water in the container to vary the resistance you feel, and you're able to monitor your workout.

The Pilate's Ball Drill

A great and simple drill to learn the "feel" of how your arms should work during the swing is to practice swinging with a pilate's exercise ball between your elbows. (The pilate's ball is about seven and one-half inches in diameter and does not have a slippery texture.) This drill emphasizes that the elbows should be a constant distance apart during the entire

The SwingWave is a good training and exercising aid.

swing. It is an easy way to cure "flying elbows" at the top of the backswing or at the finish of the swing. Try to hit some practice shots with the ball between your elbows. This is one of the least expensive and most beneficial practice aids I've ever come across.

13

Shot Making

Shot making is the ability to control the trajectory of the ball and to intentionally curve it to the left and to the right. While this involves some advanced technique, every golfer should have some knowledge of how to control the flight of the ball.

This topic brings to mind a funny story. Many, many years ago I was playing a team match on the Black Course at Bethpage Golf Club, on Long Island, the site of the 2002 U.S. Open. My partner was Jan Arden, an entertainer as well as a good golfer and a man with a lot of common sense. We were playing against two of the colorful and talented players who hung around there. The match was even at the 12th hole. Jan and our opponents all hit their second shots into the greenside bunkers. I was the last to play to the green. Since I was "the kid" in the group, Jan sauntered over for a consultation before I hit. He asked what type of shot I had in mind. I told him I was going to hit a left-to-right 6-iron, a little fade. Jan asked, "Where's the tree?" I got the hint. I shortened up on a 6-iron and hit it in the middle of the green. The lesson was learned: don't get fancy if you don't have to.

The Low Shot

Wind is a challenge golfers face all over the world. Being able to keep the ball low into the wind gives you a big edge over the competition, and it's fun to play those shots!

To hit the intentional low shot:

- Choose a club with less loft, the 7-iron instead of the 8-iron.
- Position the ball back in the stance, two to three inches.
- Use a three-quarter swing.
- Swing smoothly. The Scots have a saying: "When it's breezy, swing easy." Good idea. If you swing too hard in the breeze, you will force the club too steeply into the turf, which forces the ball up into the wind, resulting in a high, not low, trajectory.
- Use a low follow-through.

The High Shot

To hit the high shot:

- Choose a club with extra loft.
- Position the ball a little forward in the stance.
- Swing smoothly.
- Finish high.

The Hook or Draw

To hit the draw or hook, start by closing the stance (for right-handed players) so a line across the toes points to the right of the target. Slightly close the face of the club, and make a smooth swing. For a dramatic hook, rotate the toe of the club past the heel of the club. This last move is quite advanced.

The Fade or Slice

It follows that to hit the fade or slice, you open the stance (for right-handed players) so a line across the toes points to the left of the target. Slightly open the face of the club, and make a smooth swing. For a dramatic slice, hold the face of the club open a little longer, keeping the heel of the club ahead of the toe. Once again, this is quite advanced.

14

Flaws and Fixes

I thought it would be a good idea to describe a few common faults and some logical fixes for them. These nuggets might help midround if you feel your game slipping.

Topping the Ball

Topping the ball is when the player hits the very top of the ball with the very bottom of the clubhead. Because there is no loft on the very bottom of the clubhead the ball rolls along the ground. The "top" can come about in a few ways: standing too far from the ball, holding the handle of the club too tightly, or not having enough tilt at the address position. The fix is to check your posture and make sure your upper arms can touch your chest. Grip pressure should be medium light so that your arms naturally extend during the swing.

The Dreaded Slice

The slice is the most common problem among all recreational players. It is caused by an open clubface and an outside-to-inside swing path. If the slice is getting out of hand with your driver during the round, switch to the #3 metal-wood. It has less loft and therefore will produce less sidespin.

To reduce the slice, check your grip. Grip pressure should be medium light; a tight hold on the club will reduce your ability to rotate the club back to square at impact. The "V" of your top-hand grip should point toward your back shoulder.

A good drill that you can use before you swing is the baseball drill explained in Chapter 12. You can even build that drill into your preshot routine and do it every time you swing. It will reduce that old banana ball.

The Duck Hook

The duck hook, or quick hook, is a shot where the ball dives quickly left (for right-handed players). It is an out-of-control shot produced by either having an incorrect grip or swinging too fast. The cure is to first check your top-hand grip. You often get a duck hook if your top hand is moving to a "strong" position. When you look down at your grip, you should see two or maybe three knuckles. If your hand has moved over so that you can see four knuckles, you will close the clubface too fast on the downswing. Another fix for the quick hook is to soften the grip pressure, which will help you slow down your swing and get back to the correct tempo.

The Line-Drive Pitch or Chip Shot

One of the most frustrating situations in golf is when you've hit some good shots to get up to the green, only to line-drive a pitch or chip shot over the green. The "skulled" or line-drive chip or pitch is a result of hitting the ball on the very bottom of the club instead of squarely in the center of the clubface. The bottom of the clubface meets the equator of the ball so you don't get the desired loft, but rather a low line drive.

For a cure, try this:

- Soften your grip pressure so that you can feel the clubhead.
- Brush the grass with the clubhead several times before you play the stroke so that you get the feel of the clubhead staying low to the ground. A shallower swing will ensure that the loft of the clubhead lifts the ball into the air.
- Review the no-peek drill described in Chapter 12: hit the ball, keep your head steady, listen for the ball to land on the green, and look up to see the ball (hopefully) close to the pin.

15

Etiquette

Golf etiquette establishes the rules of our golf culture. The bad news is that proper etiquette will not lower your score. The good news is that it will enhance your enjoyment of the game.

Etiquette begins before you leave home. You should call in advance for a tee time. This will help ensure that you play at a desired time. Golf courses are sometimes booked with outings or a lot of play. It's so much better to discover that with a phone call than with an unnecessary trip. Leave yourself plenty of time. The toughest shot of the day is the first tee shot. Rushing to hit it makes it much more difficult.

A good way to warm up is to do some walking. You may want to park at the far end of the lot and walk the extra yards to get the blood flowing. Also, doing some of the stretches mentioned in Chapter 5 will warm up your muscles and increase flexibility.

Register in the pro shop, and always allow some extra time, as there may be other customers, and you may want to make a last-minute purchase (maybe a few extra golf balls, just in case).

When you get to the first tee, present the receipt you received from the pro shop to the starter. The starter will normally give you some of the cart rules of the day and some general information about the course.

The starter also may pair you with other players, in which case, be sure to introduce yourself to them. A good habit is to write down the name of those with whom you're paired on the scorecard. It's easy to forget names after that first handshake.

Put your mark on your ball by just making a few dots with a felt-tip pen. For the price of an inexpensive pen, you can look like a pro. And if you think you have trouble meeting people on the golf course, just pick up the wrong ball . . . you'll meet lots of people!

Wait for the group ahead of you to get well out of the way. And yell "fore!" if the ball has the slightest chance of hitting someone.

Watch your ball carefully after you hit it, so you know where it comes to rest. Line it up with a tree or something in the background. All too often, we'll hit a poor shot and look away. The poor shots are the ones we really have to watch! The goods ones are easy to find—they're in the fairway!

Your playing partners may sometimes not be familiar with golf course etiquette. They may be standing in the wrong place or jingling coins in their pockets. If that happens, mention the problem to them. No one wants to be discourteous. While a player is hitting, others in the group should stand motionless. Also, watch the flight of the ball of the other players so that you can assist them in finding an errant shot. It will help speed up play.

Pace of play is one of the most important parts of golf etiquette. All golfers hope to play a round in four hours or less. So, everyone should play at a brisk pace for the enjoyment of all. The barometer of how quickly your group is playing is how well you are keeping up with the group ahead. You cannot play any faster than the group ahead of you. If the group you are waiting for on each stroke takes four hours to play, your group also will take four hours to play.

New players face a lot of pressure to play at a good pace. Novices can still enjoy the game and play quickly by following some simple rules:

- If you've reached a score of double par and have not made the green, pick up the ball.
- Tailor long holes by starting way down the fairway.
- Play off another player's tee shot.

All golfers were new players at one time, even the experts, so everyone understands how nervous a new player can be. As long as the new players keep moving, everyone on the course can have a good day.

To give you a sense of the spirit of the game, here are the three original rules of golf:

- Play the course as you find it.
- Play the ball as it lies.
- If you can't do either of these, do what is fair.

Some courses allow you to improve how the ball lies on the fairway. This is a local rule and is normally suggested if the course is not in top condition.

Finally, cell phones should be left in the car unless, of course, you're a doctor. People play so that they can leave the office.

Etiquette in the Sand Bunkers

- Take your practice swings outside the bunker.
- Enter the bunker from the low side to prevent damage.
- Take only one club into the bunker.
- Rake bunkers after you play your shot.

Etiquette on the Green

- Locate balls of all players on the green.
- Mark your ball.
- Repair your ball mark (yours and one other). When a lofted shot lands on the green it will make a little dent in the putting surface. You should pry that dent up with a tee or repair tool. And while you're there fix one that another golfer forgot to fix. Fixed ball marks heal immediately. Ball marks that are not fixed immediately take weeks to heal.
- Don't walk in any other player's line.
- Don't cast a shadow in someone's line.
- Putt out at a good pace.
- The player who is closest to the hole is responsible for tending or removing the flagstick.
- The last person to putt out should replace the flagstick.

Etiquette with Golf Carts

- Place your clubs behind where you plan to sit.
- Observe cart rules for the day. If it's "cart paths only," then all four tires should be on the cart path at all times.
- When you leave the cart to play your stroke, take several clubs.
- Never drive the cart within 60 feet of the green.
- At the green, park the cart on the way to the next green.
- Write down scores at, or on the way to, the next tee.

Golf etiquette is based on a lot of common sense and the shared idea that for the enjoyment of all, golf should be played at a brisk pace.

16

Some Final Thoughts

We all want to hit the ball consistently. Remember that balance is the key to solid contact.

Keep it simple. We can easily become confused about the golf swing. Stay away from quick fixes. Stick to the proven fundamentals; they always work.

Play at a good pace. Golfers seem to either speed up or slow down when they become seniors. I don't know why. Playing at a fairly quick pace makes the game more enjoyable for all. Line up your next stroke as your playing partners are hitting theirs. Be ready to play when it's your turn. Golfers who play at a good pace are asked for a game much more often than slowpokes.

There is nothing quite like golf. It's a game that presents us an infinite amount of fun and challenges. It provides the strong player the chance to hit the ball farther than anyone else. It provides those with finesse the chance to develop a short game that can more than make up for any lack of power. You even get to wear great clothes. And, of course, it's a game that no one can master.

In golf we can get just the right amount of exercise to keep us healthy. And the golf course is such a wonderful place to meet new friends and enjoy old ones. So, swing away and have fun!

It was my purpose in this book to pass on some of the things I've learned through the years and how I've carried those experiences to my play as a senior. I hope I've offered some suggestions that will improve your senior golf. That would make me very happy.

Glossary

Ace: A hole scored in one stroke. Also known as a "hole in one."

Addressing the ball: Taking a stance by placing one's feet in position for and in preparation of making a stroke and also grounding the club. In a hazard, taking a stance in preparation of making a stroke.

All square: An even score, neither side being a hole up.

Approach: A stroke or shot to the putting green.

Apron: The last few yards of fairway in front of the green.

Away: The farthest from the hole.

Backspin: Backward rotation of the ball, causing it to stop abruptly.

Bent grass: A species of grass used for putting greens.

Best ball: A match in which a single player competes against the best ball of two or more players.

Birdie: One stroke under par for a hole.

Blind: An approach position from which the green cannot be seen.

Bogey: One stroke over par for a hole.

Borrow or break: In putting, to play to either side of the direct line from the ball to the hole to compensate for roll or slant in the green.

Bunker: An area of bare ground, often a marked depression, usually covered with sand.

Bye holes: Holes remaining after a match is finished, that is, after one side is more holes up than remain for play.

Caddie: A person who carries a player's clubs.

Carry: The distance from where a ball is hit to where it first strikes the ground.

Casual water: Any temporary accumulation of water, such as a puddle after rain.

Chip: A short approach shot on which the ball flies close to the ground (compare with "Pitch").

Concede: To grant that an opponent has won a hole before play has been completed.

Course: The terrain over which the game is played; the whole area within which play is permitted.

Cup: The hole into which the ball is played, measuring four and one-half inches in diameter and at least four inches deep.

Default: To concede a match to an opponent without playing against the opponent; also, to fail to appear for a scheduled match.

Divot: A piece of grass cut out by a club during a stroke. Divots should always be replaced before the player moves on.

Dogleg: A hole that bends sharply to the left or right between the tee and the green.

Down: In match play, a side's having lost more holes than it has won.

Draw: A controlled hook.

Dub: An unskillful player; also, to hit the ball poorly.

Eagle: Two strokes under par for a hole.

Face: The slope of a bunker; also, the part of the clubhead that strikes the ball.

Fade: A controlled slice.

Fairway: The closely cut turf intended for play between the tee and the green.

Flagstick: A movable straight indicator, usually a lightweight pole with a numbered flag, placed in the hole to show its location; sometimes referred to as the pin.

Follow-through: Continuation of the swing of the club after the ball has been struck.

"Fore!" A warning cry by a player to any person in the way of the ball.

Forecaddie: A person employed to indicate the position of balls on the course.

Four-ball match: A match in which there are two players to a side, each side playing its better ball against the better ball of the other side.

Foursome: A match in which there are two players to a side, each side playing one ball.

Green: The putting green or very closely mown area around the cup.

Gross: A player's score before deduction of any handicap.

Ground: To rest the club lightly on the ground in preparing to strike the ball. To touch the ground behind the ball with the clubhead before you begin the swing.

Ground under repair: Any portion of the course under repair or maintenance. If a ball should land on ground under repair, or if the ground under repair should interfere with a player's stance or swing, the ball may be lifted and dropped, without penalty, as near as possible to where it lay, but not nearer the hole.

Halved: The situation when each side has taken the same number of strokes on a hole.

Handicap: The number of strokes a player receives to adjust his or her score to a common level, the generally accepted common level being scratch, or zero-handicap, golf.

Hanging: Lying on a downslope.

Hazard: Any bunker or water hazard.

Heel: The part of the clubhead nearest the shaft; also, to hit from this part and send the ball at right angles to the line of play.

Hole: The cup into which the ball is played; also, one of the 18 units on a course, consisting of teeing ground, fairway, rough, hazards, and putting green.

Hole-high: A ball that lies even with the hole but to one side.

Hole out: To make the final stroke in playing the ball into the hole.

Honor: The privilege of driving off, or playing from, the teeing ground first.

Hook: To curve the ball widely to the left.

Hosel: The socket on the clubhead into which the shaft is fitted.

Lateral water hazard: A water hazard running approximately parallel to the line of play and so situated that it is impractical to keep the spot at which a ball crosses the hazard margin between the player and the hole. A water hazard, lake, stream, etc., that is alongside the fairway.

Lie: The inclination of a club when held on the ground in the natural position for striking; also, the situation of the ball.

Line: The direction in which a player desires the ball to travel.

Links: A golf course, especially a seaside course.

Loft: To elevate the ball; also, the backward slant of the face of the club.

Long game: The strokes in which obtaining distance is more important than accuracy.

Loose impediment: A natural object not fixed or growing, such as a stone, leaf, or twig.

Marker: A scorer in stroke play appointed by a tournament committee to record a competitor's score; also, an indicator of the front edge of a teeing ground or the boundaries of a hole.

Match play: Reckoning the score by holes won and lost.

Medal play: Stroke play.

Mixed foursome: A foursome in which a man and a woman play as partners.

Nassau: A system of scoring under which one point is awarded for winning the first 9 holes, one for the second 9, and a third for the full 18.

Net: A player's score after deduction of any handicap.

Observer: A person appointed by a tournament committee to assist a referee in deciding questions of fact and to report to the referee any breach of a rule.

Obstruction: Anything artificial that has been erected, placed, or left on the course.

Out of bounds: Ground on which play is prohibited.

Outside agency: A referee, an observer, a marker, a forecaddie, or another person not a part of the match or, in stroke play, not a part of a player's side.

Par: Theoretically perfect play, or the score an expert would be expected to make on a hole, determined by the number of strokes required to reach the green plus two putts. Par is calculated on the basis of distance. Women's par for a course is slightly higher than par for men. United States Golf Association standards for computing par are as follows:

	Men's Par	Women's Par
Par 3	up to 250 yards	up to 210 yards
Par 4	251 to 470 yards	211 to 400 yards
Par 5	471 yards and over	401 to 575 yards
Par 6	576 yards and over	

Penalty stroke: A stroke added to the score of a side under certain rules.

Pin: A rod or pole to which a flag is attached (see "Flagstick").

Pitch: An approach shot on which the ball is lofted in a high arc (compare with "Chip").

Pitch and run: An approach shot on which a part of the desired distance is covered by the roll of the ball after it strikes the ground.

Pivot: The turn of the body as a stroke is played.

Pull: To hit the ball so that it will curve to the left.

Putt: A stroke made on a putting green.

Putting green: All ground of the hole being played that is specially prepared for putting or is otherwise defined as such by the committee.

Referee: A person appointed by the tournament committee to accompany players to decide questions of fact and rules of golf.

Rough: Long grass bordering the fairway and also, at times, between the tee and the fairway; may include bushes, trees, and so forth.

Rub of the green: Any deflection or stoppage of a ball by an outside agency; the ball is played as it lies, without penalty.

Run: To hit a ball along the ground in an approach instead of chipping or pitching it; also, the distance a ball rolls after it lands.

Sand trap: A bunker having a layer of sand.

Scratch player: One who receives no handicap allowance.

Short game: Approach shots and putts.

Single: A match between two players.

Slice: To curve the ball widely to the right.

Square: The stage at which a match is even.

Stance: The position of the feet and body when a player is addressing the ball.

Stroke: Forward movement of the club with the intention of fairly striking the ball.

Stroke hole: A hole on which a handicap stroke is given.

Stroke play: Also known as medal play. Both are defined as the amount of strokes it takes to complete the given number of holes. Usually 18, but often 9 holes.

Tee: An artificial peg or a pinch of sand on which the ball may be placed for the first stroke on each hole.

Teeing ground: The starting place for the hole to be played, indicated by two marks on the ground; also called the tee.

Three-ball match: A match in which three players compete against one another, each playing his or her own ball.

Threesome: A match in which one player competes against two, who play alternate strokes with the same ball.

Through the green: The whole area of the course except hazards and the teeing ground and putting green of the hole being played.

Up: In match play, a side's having won more holes than it has lost.

Water hazard: Any water (except casual water) or water course, regardless of whether it contains water. An area so marked as a water hazard. Penalty for a ball hit into a water hazard is one stroke.

Bibliography

Graham, Lou, with Desmond Tolhurst. *Top Tips from Senior Golfers.* New York: Simon & Schuster, 1990.

Hogan, Ben. *Ben Hogan's Five Lessons: The Modern Fundamentals of Golf.* New York: Pocket Books, 1990.

Penick, Harvey. *Harvey Penick's Little Red Book: Lessons and Teachings From a Lifetime of Golf.* New York: Simon & Schuster, 1999.

Roberts, Katherine. *Yoga for Golfers: A Unique Mind-Body Approach to Golf Fitness.* New York: McGraw-Hill, 2004.

Shapiro, Alan. *Golf's Mental Hazards: Overcome Them and Put an End to the Self-Destructive Round.* New York: Fireside, 1996.

Index

Abdominal bicycle exercise, 77
Achilles tendon/shoulders
    combination stretch, 50
Address position, golf swing, 8–11
Aerobics, 48
Alcohol, 84
Arnot, Bob, 84
Arrival
    course management, 21–22
    tournaments, 32

Back stretch, 51
Bad-weather golf, 31
Ball above feet, 27
Ball below feet, 27–28
Ball buried against front of bunker
    shot, 110
Ball exercises, 56–65
    biceps curls, 58
    crunches, 61
    dumbbell chest press, 57
    dumbbell row, 57
    dumbbell shoulder press, 61
    front deltoid raise, 62
    hammer curls, 64
    knee extension, 60
    lateral deltoid raise, 62–63
    leg curls, 60
    lying triceps, 58–59
    rear deltoid raise, 63

    reverse wrist curls, 64–65
    standing calf raise, 59
    wrist curls, 64–65
Ball toss, 132
Balls, golf, 40
Baseball drill, 124–25
Belly putter, 101
Biceps curls, 58
Biceps stretch, 50–51
Blood sugar, 82–83
Bones, and physical conditioning,
    78–79
Breathing, and tournaments, 34
Bunker shots, 106–9
Buried lies shot, 108–9

Caffeine, and tournaments, 32
Calf stretch, 49
Cardiovascular
    conditioning/aerobics, 48
Chest stretch, 50
Chip shot flaws, 140–41
Claw putting grip, 101–2
Clean lies shot, 106–8
Cocchi, Jim, 45
Coin drill, 127
Confidence, 44
Course management, 21–34
    arrive early, 21–22
    bad-weather golf, 31

ball above feet, 27
ball below feet, 27–28
deep grass, 30
distances, 30–31
downhill lie, 28–29
flight pattern, 23
launching pad, 29–30
practice holes, 22–26
sidehill lie, 27–28
tee box, 23–24
tournaments, 31–34
uneven courses, 26–30
uphill lie, 29–30
Cross-handed method, putting,
    101
Crunches, 61, 76

Deep grass course management, 30
Distances, course management,
    30–31
Downhill bunker shot, 109–10
Downhill lie, course management,
    28–29
Downhill putts, 100
Downswing, 14–15
Draw shot, 136
Dreaded slice flaws, 140
Drills, 121–33
    baseball drill, 124–25
    coin drill, 127
    emergency drill, 125–26
    feet-together drill, 124
    no-peek drill, 127–28
    preset drill, 125
    sand drill, 126–27
    split-grip drill, 123–24
    step-through drill, 125
    toe-up, toe-up drill, 123
Duck hook flaws, 140
Dumbbell chest press, 57
Dumbbell exercises, 66–77

Dumbbell row, 57
Dumbbell shoulder press, 61
Dumbbell squat, 66

Eating, and tournaments, 32
Els, Ernie, 18
Emergency drill, 125–26
Equipment, 35–40
    balls, 40
    grip, 37
    irons, 38
    lob wedge, 38
    long-distance drivers, 39–40
    metal-woods, 38
    recommendations, 37–40
    shaft, 36
    women players, 115–16
Etiquette, 143–46
    golf cart, 146
    on green, 145
    sand bunkers, 145

Fade shot, 137
Fairway bunkers, 111–12
Feet-together drill, 124
Feldstein, Larry, 47
Flaws, 139–41
    chip shot, 140–41
    dreaded slice, 140
    duck hook, 140
    line-drive pitch, 140–41
    topping ball, 139
Flexibility, and physical
    conditioning, 48, 79–80
Flight pattern, course management,
    23
Flop shot, 90–92
Food, women players and, 115
Forearm stretch, 55
Forearms stretch, 56
Front deltoid raises, 62

Golf cart, etiquette, 146
Golf grip, 3–7
Golf myths, 117–19
   head down, 117–18
   left arm pull down, 119
   left arm straight, 118–19
Golf performance and physical
   conditioning, 78
Golf swing, 1–19
   address position, 8–11
   golf grip, 3–7
   preshot routine, 1–3
   releasing the club, 18
   tempo, 18–19
   waggle, 11–12
Golf's Mental Hazards (Shapiro),
   42
Grass, deep management, 30
Green, Hubert, vii, 45–46
Grips, 37
   tournaments, 34

Hammer curls, 64
Hamstring stretch, 52–53
Hardpan playing, 94
Haroutunian, Harry, 81
Head down golf myths, 117–18
High shot, 136
Hinge, 4
Hogan, Ben, 43
Hook shot, 136

Impact bag, 130–32
Incline biceps curls, 72–73
Irons, 38

Jones, Bobby, 18–19

Knee extension, 60
Knees flex, 10
Kroll, Ted, 41

Lat pull-down, 70–71
Lateral deltoid raises, 62–63
Launching pad, course management,
   29–30
Left arm pull down myth, 119
Left arm straight myth, 118–19
Leg curls, 60, 68
Leg extension, 67
Line-drive pitch flaws, 140–41
Listening trick, putting, 100
Lob wedge, 38
Long-distance drivers, 39–40
Long greenside bunker shot, 110–11
Long putter, 101
Long putts with break, 99
Low shot, 136
Lower-back exercise, 74–75
Lying chest press, 70
Lying triceps, 58–59

Machine exercises, 66–77
Machine shoulder press, 72–73
Maiden, Stewart, 18
Massage, physical conditioning and,
   48
Medicus, 129
Mental game, 41–46
Mental toughness, 43–44
Metal-woods, 38
Newell, Susanne, 115

Nicklaus, Jack, 43
No-peek drill, 127–28
Nutrition, 81–84
   blood sugar, 82–83

On green etiquette, 145
Osteoporosis, 79

Pec dec, 72
Pelz Putting Track, 132

Physical challenges, recovery from, 45–46
Physical conditioning, 47–80
  bones, 78–79
  cardiovascular conditioning/aerobics, 48
  flexibility, 48, 79–80
  golf performance and, 78
  massage, 48
  strength, 47–48, 79–80
  stretches, 48–56
Pilate's ball drill, 133
Pitching, 87–89
Posture, 3, 10
Practice
  course management, 22–26
  tournaments, 31–32, 34
  women players, 116
Preparation, tournaments, 32
Preset drill, 125
Preshot routine, 1–3
Price, Nick, 18
Proper aim, putting, 96–97
Putting, 95–103
  belly putter, 101
  claw putting grip, 101–2
  cross-handed method, 101
  developing feel, 97–98
  downhill putts, 100
  listening trick, 100
  long putter, 101
  long putts with break, 99
  proper aim, 96–97
  slow greens, 100
  strategies, 99–100
  yips, 102–3

Quad stretches, 51–52

Rear deltoid raises, 63
Recommendations, equipment, 37–40

Recovery from physical challenges, 45–46
Releasing the club swing, 18
Reverse curls, 74–75
Reverse wrist curls, 64–65
Rotator cuff stretch, 54

Sand bunkers etiquette, 145
Sand drill, 126–27
Sand game, 105–12
  ball buried against front of bunker, 110
  bunker shots, 106–9
  buried lies shot, 108–9
  clean lies shot, 106–8
  downhill bunker shot, 109–10
  fairway bunkers, 111–12
  long greenside bunker shot, 110–11
  sand wedge, 106
Sand wedge shot, 106
Seated cable row, 71
Shaft, 36
Shapiro, Alan, 42
Short game, 85–103
  flop shot, 90–92
  hardpan playing, 94
  pitching, 87–89
  shots from apron, 85–87
  stroke savers, 92–94
  Texas wedge, 90
Shot making, 135–37
  fade or slice, 137
  high shot, 136
  hook or draw, 136
  low shot, 136
Shots from apron, 85–87
Side bends, 54
Sidehill lie, course management, 27–28
Slice shot, 137, 140
Slow greens, putting, 100

Snead, Sam, 23
Speed, swing, 18–19
Split-grip drill, 123–24
Standing calf raise, 59
Standing one-leg calf raise, 69
Staying in the game, 44
Step-through drill, 125
Strength, physical conditioning and,
        47–48, 79–80
Strength, women players, 116
Stretches, 48–56
Stroke savers, 92–94
Sugary snacks, tournaments, 33
Swing speed, 18–19
SwingWave, 133

Teaching aids, 128–33
    ball toss, 132
    impact bag, 130–32
    Medicus, 129
    Pelz Putting Track, 132
    pilate's ball drill, 133
    SwingWave, 133
    video/DVD, 128–29
    weighted driver, 129–30
Tee box, course management,
        23–24
Tempo, golf swing, 18–19
Texas wedge, 90
Toe-up, toe-up drill, 123
Topping ball flaws, 139
Tournaments, 31–34
    arrival, 32
    breathing, 34
    caffeine, 32

eating, 32
grip, 34
practice green, 34
practice rounds, 31–32
preparation, 32
sugary snacks, 33
warm-up, 33–34
Triceps press-down, 74
Triceps stretch, 53
Twists, 54–55

Uneven courses, 26–30
United States Golf Association, 39,
        40
Uphill lie, course, 29–30

V grip, 5–7
Vardon grip, 6
Video/DVD teaching aids, 128–29

Waggle, golf swing, 11–12
Warm-up, tournaments, 33–34
Water, 84
Weighted driver, 129–30
Women players, 113–19
    equipment, 115–16
    flaws, 114–15
    food, 115
    practice, 116
    strength, 116
Woods, Tiger, 43–44
Wrist curls, 64–65
Wrist stretch, 55

Yips, putting, 102–3

About the Author

Jay Morelli is founder and current director of The Original Golf School, which has three locations: Mount Snow, Vermont; Ocean City, Maryland; and Crystal River, Florida. This program has graduated almost 100,000 adult students since it was started in 1978. He has written two other books: *Beginning Golf*, published by Sterling, and *The Original Golf School Way*, published by Schoolhouse Press. He has also written a golf instruction manual for the school's students as well as numerous newspaper and magazine articles on golf tips. In addition, he has produced two instructional videos.

Morelli has won numerous awards in professional golf, including Teacher of the Year for the New England PGA, *Golf Digest*—Best Teacher in the State Award, *Golf Digest*—One of the Best Teachers in New England Award, and twice Vermont PGA Golf Professional of the Year.

He has excellent playing credentials, too. As an amateur, he won the Long Island and New York State high school championships and attended Florida State University on a golf scholarship. As a professional, he won the Northeastern New York PGA championship, was twice a medalist in the U.S. Open qualifier (local), and twice won the Vermont PGA Pro-Pro championship.